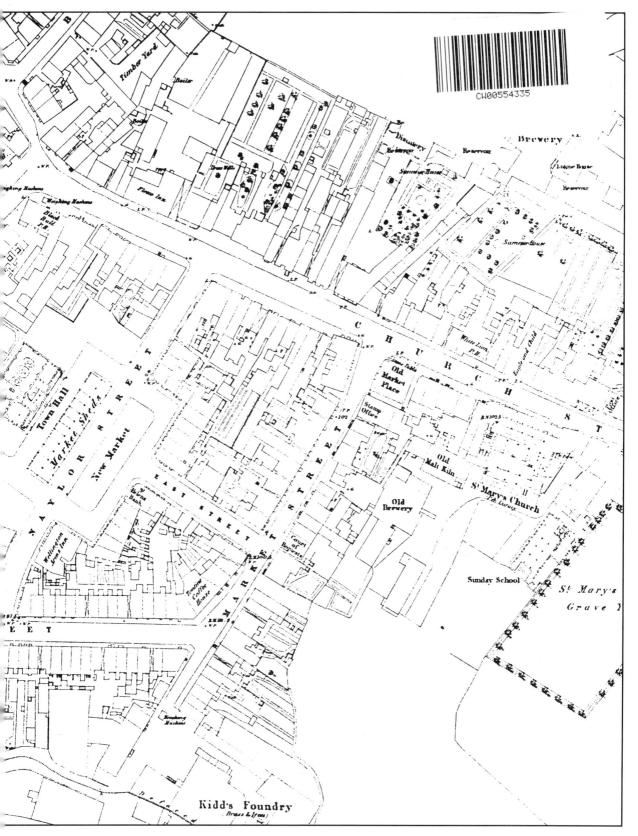

St Helens Town Centre in 1849. (Extract from Sheet 4, 60-inch O.S. map, size reduced.)

ST HELENS
A Pictorial History

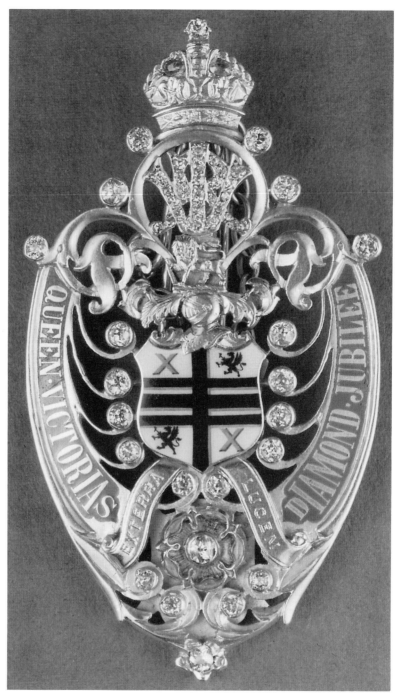

The Mayoress's jewel, worn on her chain of office, was presented to St Helens by Richard Pilkington, the then mayor, on 22 June 1897, to mark Queen Victoria's Diamond Jubilee. Diamonds sparkle in the royal monogram, above the Borough's Coat of Arms and motto 'Ex terra Lucem ...' [from the earth light ...]. Below is the red rose of Lancashire. The arms of the four townships' leading manorial families combine to form the shield. The two bars of the Parrs lie under the cross of the Ecclestons. Quartered are the diagonal cross of the Gerards (Windle) and the griffin of the Bolds (Sutton). All remain part of the arms of St Helens Metropolitan Borough. St Helens' motto is now 'Prosperitas in Excelsis'.

ST HELENS
A Pictorial History

Mary Presland

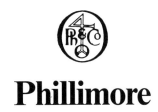

Phillimore

1995

Published by
PHILLIMORE & CO. LTD.
Shopwyke Manor Barn, Chichester, West Sussex

ISBN 0 85033 987 1

Printed and bound in Great Britain by
BIDDLES & CO. LTD.
Guildford, Surrey

For Margaret Gundry
Lancastrian, mentor and friend

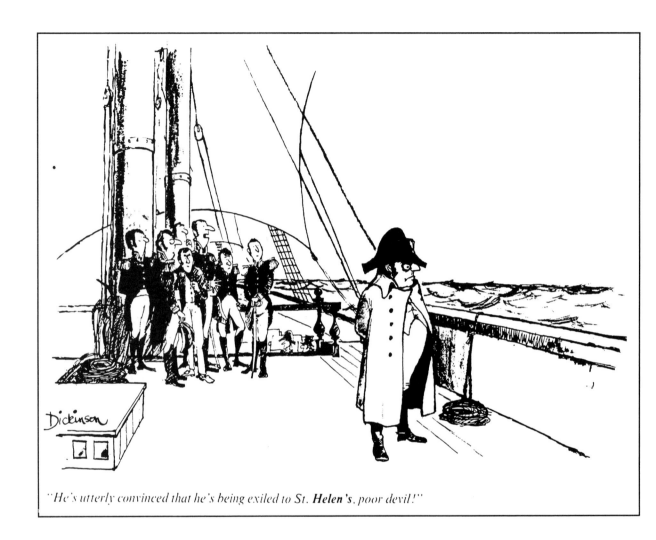

"*He's utterly convinced that he's being exiled to St.* **Helen's***, poor devil!*"

List of Illustrations

Frontispiece: The Mayoress's jewel

Acknowledgements

The author and the research team would like to thank Mrs. Vivien Hainsworth, Local History and Archives Librarian, and her colleagues at the St Helens Local History and Archive Library for their unfailing helpfulness during the preparation of this book. The Library was the source of the originals of many of the photographs and other illustrations, and particular thanks are due to Peter Sargeant, one of its staff, for making copies of them. Our thanks go also to Roger Hart, St Helens Tourism, Heritage and Events Manager, for his help and guidance, and to Pat Jones of St Helens Museum for reproducing material from the museum's collection. We thank the friends who lent us photographs and, within the group, special thanks are owed to Dorothy Hughes for converting the author's manuscript into word-processed legibility.

Our thanks for permission to use items from their collections go to: Age Concern, St Helens, 184; Grosvenor Housing Association, 89, 90; Huyton Central Library, 10; Lancashire Record Office, 2; National Museums and Galleries on Merseyside, 33; National Railway Museum, 28; National Tramways Museum, 129-130; Pilkington plc, 6-8, 57-8, 60, 122, 172, 173; St Helens Museum, 9, 12, 16, 28, 59, 74, 82, 110; *St Helens Reporter*, 38-9, 177; St Helens Sutton Athletic Club, 160; SmithKline Beecham, 78-81; Society of Friends, St Helens, 159; Y.M.C.A., St Helens, 163 and to: Mrs. A. Challoner, 176; Mr. A. Davies, 3; Mr. G. Drought, 37; Mr. J. Giblin, 92, 178; Mr. T. Glover, 167; Mr. W. Highcock, 21-4, 36, 86, 114, 144; Miss M. Irwin, 96, 126, 166; the Misses B. and G. Jones, 97-101; Mr. D. Knowles, 107, 154, 165; Mr. G. Orme, 185; Mr. A. Perrian, 69; Mr. J. Peden, 41; Mr. K. Read, 48; Mr. A. Rothwell, 29; Mr. J. Ryan, 67-8, 168; Mr. J. Tyrer, 136-7; Mr. A. Wallace, 19, 142; Mrs. N. Yearsley, 116.

We particularly thank the St Helens Local History and Archive Library, which made almost 100 items available to us, including those from the Borrows Collection, 40, the Forster's Collection, 63-4, and—with permission from Mrs. P. Eden—the Ashcroft Collection, 20, 43, 47, 61, 95. The map in the Introduction is reproduced by courtesy of the Historic Society of Lancashire and Cheshire. The remaining items 5, 118 and 182 were supplied by the author.

Introduction

Whilst some locations were well suited for settlement by man and for communities to grow, the area within which St Helens was to develop had no such apparent advantages. It stood on no major land route, nor beside a river crossing. It had no defensive merits, nor was its soil readily cultivable.

Instead it lay in a wide flat hollow south of the final outliers of the Pennines and north of the Mersey, towards which its silty watercourses ran. Boulder clay, left by ice sheets and subsequently overlaid in parts by peat mosses and, to the north, by Shirdley Hill sand, lined the hollow. Below, or sometimes outcropping, and typically slanting downwards to the south east, the remains of tropical forests lay compressed over time into coal and interspersed with layers of mudstone and sandstone. Away to the south newer sandstone beds overlay the rapidly deepening coal measures.

No Roman, looking westwards from the road to Carlisle, was tempted to linger and build a villa. There were other settlers, though, who left, in place names, clues about themselves and their surroundings.

Celts named the Sankey as a holy river; they gave 'eccles' to Eccleston, referring to a Christian religious site—perhaps an early Prescot church. By 'leah' (our 'ley'), the Angles meant a clearing. Did their cattle graze in one at Cowley, or had they found coal in open ground there? What they grew at Peasley is clear. 'Parr' was their term for fenced off ground, whilst Windleshaw identified a copse on that windy hill, Windle. They described marshy ground as 'moss'. The 'carr' of Carr Mill was the equivalent for Norse settlers, whose word for a hut or shelter lingers at Scholes. By Laffak (law-oak) they identified the tree which was the local assembly point.

The medieval traveller, following the Roman route from London to Carlisle, by crossing the Mersey at Warrington, would have entered what the compilers of Domesday Book called 'the land between the Ribble and the Mersey'. In 1086, this part of the future county of Lancashire largely consisted of royal estates, with each administrative division, or hundred, based on a royal manor, a possible reason for the brevity of detail entered in Domesday. Warrington, Newton and, within (West) Derby hundred, Skelmersdale, Aughton, Wavertree and Speke were named, but in the area they encircled, where St Helens was later to develop, no settlement received mention.

Townships had come into being as minor civil units within the hundreds well before Domesday. They were grouped for ecclesiastical purposes into the characteristically large Lancashire parishes. The townships of Eccleston, Windle, Parr and Sutton (the mystery place—of what was this 'tun'/enclosure south?) and 11 others constituted Prescot parish. This was the largest of the 16 parishes in (West) Derby hundred and, like all other parishes between the Ribble and the Mersey, had since the tenth century been part of the diocese of Lichfield.

In these huge parishes—Prescot parish extended to Rainford in the north, Burtonwood in the east and Widnes in the south—chapels of ease were created to save long journeys to parish churches. Such a chapel was built in Hardshaw, a district within Windle, beside the road from Warrington to Ormskirk, a little beyond the turning for Bolton and just before it was joined by the road from Prescot. It was dedicated to St Helen—mother of Constantine the Great—and is shown as 'Sct Elyns Chap:' on Saxton's map of Lancashire of 1579.

Thomas Parre of Parre, in his will of 1558, had given 'tenne shelynges to be a stocke towardes fyndynge of a preest at Sainct Elyns Chapell in Hardshae [sic] and to the mayntenance of Goddes devyne service there for ever if the stocke goe forthwarde and that a priest doe service as is aforsaid'. Six years earlier an inventory had listed only a little bell and a chalice as having been owned by the chapel. In their deed of 1613 Katherine and James Downbell placed the chapel in the hands of local trustees, responsible for appointing a priest and for maintenance of the fabric, 'that the same now being in great decay may be repaired'.

The scarcity of goods and funds and the decay of the building suggest a sparse and not very affluent population, an impression confirmed half a century later. The Hearth Tax Returns for 1662 for the four townships, which covered an area almost 40 per cent larger than the Borough that was to be created in 1868, revealed hearths in only 323 locations—an average of about one dwelling per 28 acres. Almost half those listed had just one hearth and about a third only two. By contrast, Hardshaw, Parr and Eltonhead Halls had six, seven and eight hearths respectively, while Eccleston Hall possessed twenty-four.

Of course, the Hearth Tax Lists may be regarded only as an approximate guide to population, as there were exemptions from the tax, such as industrial hearths (other than smiths' forges and bakers' ovens) and those of charitable institutions (e.g. the school attached to St Elyn's Chapel), and of the lowliest inhabitants—persons in receipt of poor relief or in property worth less than 20s. per annum. But, undoubtedly, dependence largely on agriculture in an area interspersed with heaths and mosses meant that the four townships remained thinly populated until well into the 18th century.

Yet certainly by 1540 the townships' great latent source of wealth had been discovered. Coal was then being mined at Sutton Heath, barely two miles from St Elyn's Chapel, according to a witness in a legal dispute of 1580 concerning rights to this now valuable land. Mining had also been established at Burtonhead where an estate plan of about 1580 identified one area as 'Pemb[er]tons Cole Mynes'. Pits were usually shallow—worked, where the seam outcropped, by a few men, a family perhaps, with minimal equipment—ladders, ropes, buckets, baskets, picks, a sieve, possibly a windlass. The extent of the workings depended on the strength of the rock beds between which the coal seams lay and the rapidity with which water permeated the site. As one pit became unworkable, a new one would be dug close by, creating the pock-marked land surface depicted on the Burtonhead plan.

Though simple to extract from the earth, coal was difficult to transport from the pits—moving it 10 miles overland could increase its price five-fold. Turves cut from the mosses met many local needs for fuel and one wonders on how many of the hearths listed in 1662 coal was used. For mining to expand, there had not only to be a demand for coal, but also a means of supplying it where demanded at an acceptable price.

Across the Mersey, in Cheshire, 'white' salt had been refined since Roman times and sent to neighbouring counties. Brine naturally occurred in springs and underground lakes and was made into salt by evaporation, a fuel-greedy process. The nearest Lancashire coal, arriving by packhorse, having been shipped across the river to Frodsham Bridge, was in 1698 said to cost 16s. 8d. a ton at Northwich. At this time a Lancashire building worker was earning about 8d. a day.

By then, an unsuccessful attempt to find coal in Cheshire had led instead to the discovery, at Marbury, of rock salt deposits. If rock salt was immersed in large chambers (preferably using salt-water) it would dissolve. The resultant brine could be pumped out and evaporated. Rock salt works were set up at Dungeon (Hale), where in 1698 coal cost only 5s. 6d. per ton, at Frodsham and in Liverpool (hence Salthouse Dock). Rock salt was also being shipped from Liverpool.

Earlier, in 1666, on the first recorded there-and-back transatlantic voyage from Liverpool, *Antelope* had sailed for Barbados carrying 'white' salt and coal, though her main cargo was linen cloth. She returned with raw sugar for boiling in Liverpool's first sugar refinery. At that date, Liverpool had seven streets, 300 houses and about 1,500 inhabitants. Other and larger vessels followed *Antelope*'s example and by 1709 streets and population had quadrupled. Liverpool's mayor claimed it to be England's third port (after London and Bristol) and Defoe called it 'one of the wonders of Britain'. By 1715 its first dock was completed.

All was not idyllic. Liverpool grew increasingly short of coal for its citizens' hearths, for its breweries, potteries, sugar refineries and salt-works and also for cargo for its growing merchant fleet.

Prescot's pits lay closest, but on a road such that coals could only be brought in during good summer weather. No wonder it was Liverpool merchants who in 1726 obtained an Act of Parliament to help put matters right. The road from Low Hill to Prescot was to be turnpiked, and carriers of coal to pay preferentially low rates. (The reverse applied to earthenware, seen as a threat to Liverpool enterprises.)

This highway was, according to the Act, part of 'the ancient road from the said Town and Port of Liverpoole to the Borough of Wigan ... Halifax ... York ... ' and of 'the common post road through Warrington to London'.

Twenty years later a further Act was needed, and this time 'the chapel of St Helen, in the hamlet of Hardshaw in the Township of Windle' was specifically mentioned. Coal stocks at Prescot could not meet Liverpool's demands, and the road from Prescot to St Helens Chapel was now to be turnpiked because ' ... the amending of the said Road from Prescot to the chapel of Saint Helen, (which leads to several Coal Pits, and to the Market Towns of Bolton and Rochdale ...) and keeping the same in good Repair, will be ... a means of supplying the inhabitants (now very numerous) and also the shipping in the said Port, with great Quantities of Coals'.

Owners of coal pits close to the turnpike in Eccleston and Windle at last had access to the Liverpool market. Seven years later (1753) a further Act permitted the road from St Helens Chapel to Ashton-in-Makerfield and that from Prescot to Bank Hall, Warrington (now Warrington Town Hall), to be turnpiked, each linking with the existing Warrington-Wigan-Preston turnpike.

Local communications were improving, but even turnpiked roads could be appalling. The time of the great road builders had yet to arrive. An increase in Prescot coal prices to fund a steam pumping engine, and a new toll on empty waggons on their return journeys, prompted Liverpool's merchants to action.

It was the era of river improvement, or 'navigation', of dredging shallows, cutting across meanders, replacing fords with bridges and even bypassing weirs with 'pound' locks. The navigation of the Weaver upstream to Winsford in 1733 was spectacularly boosting the salt trade. The Mersey and Irwell had been made navigable in the 1730s and the Douglas in 1742. It was time to investigate the potential of that humble watercourse, the Sankey Brook.

A survey was needed if the petition for an Act of Parliament to permit the navigation was to succeed. Henry Berry, highway surveyor and overseer of the poor in Parr as a young man, was one of the two surveyors appointed. He was an ideal choice. He knew the area well and as clerk to Thomas Steers, Liverpool's first Dock Engineer, had worked with him on the Newry Canal. After Steers' death, when he was appointed his successor, he had completed the Salthouse Dock.

The petition succeeded and on 20 March 1755 Parliament passed 'An act for making navigable the River or Brook called *Sankey Brook*, and the Three several Branches thereof, from the River *Mersey* below *Sankey Bridges*, up to *Boardman's* Stone Bridge on the South Branch, to *Gerard's* Bridge on the Middle Branch thereof, and to *Penny Bridge* on the North Branch thereof ...' (the italicisation appears on the original document).

Whilst, to assist the Bill's passage, Berry had assured the Parliamentary Committee that navigation was possible, either then or by the time the twisting stretch below Sankey Bridges had been 'navigated', he had realised the impracticability of expecting vessels to negotiate the winding and unreliable brook. Allowed by the Act to 'dig, cut ... the said lands ... for the effecting and carrying out the said Navigation ... as the Undertakers ... shall think requisite', Henry Berry's 'cut' ran from Sankey Bridges to Penny, Boardman's and Gerard's Bridges. He had created England's first modern canal—an entirely separate channel filled with still water—constructed close to the Sankey Brook, whose water supplied its needs and accepted any overflow from it. Nine locks raised the level 80 feet from Sankey Bridges to Parr, site of the country's first double lock.

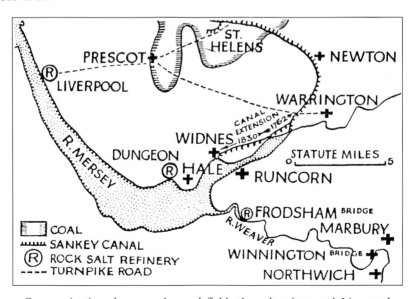

Communications between the coal field, the salt mines and Liverpool.

An effective route had been created for coal to reach the Mersey. No wonder the owners of the Dungeon and Liverpool saltworks had been prominent promoters of the navigation. No wonder Sarah Clayton, of Parr Hall, had shrewdly raised coal from new delfs even before the canal reached Parr. She advertised it in December 1757 at 'somewhat less' than the 4s. 2d. per ton of her newly mined coal, and 14 months later offered coal in Liverpool at 7s. 6d. to householders, and to ships at 7s. a ton. By now the Lancashire building labourer could expect to earn around 11d. a day.

By 1771 an estimated 90,000 tons of coal were passing down the canal, which had been extended northwards towards Laffak, and from Sankey Bridges to Fidlers Ferry. Two years later, when the branch from the New Double Lock near Gerards Bridge had reached Hardshaw and Ravenhead (Canal Street now occupies its final length), Scots-born coal proprietor John Mackay was offering excellent smiths' coal for shipping to America at 8s. 4d. a ton—the equivalent of about six days' wages.

Such sales did not content Mackay. Far-sighted, he saw the value of attracting furnace industries to his coal-rich canal-served Ravenhead properties. His successes largely called modern St Helens into being.

For at least half a century, glass bottles had been made at Thatto Heath; some had been brought to Nicholas Blundell from there in June 1721. Now, thanks to Mackay's wealthy London business connections, England's largest industrial building of the period—the British Cast Plate Glass Company's Manufactory—was built at Ravenhead. Mackay's coal heated its furnaces and the molten glass was poured on to rectangular casting tables. Cooled, ground and polished, it glazed the houses and coaches of the wealthy, or, silvered, became their mirrors.

The canal was used to send off the company's products to London, their main market. It was used, too, to bring in a new raw material—copper ore from Anglesey.

Tempted by the price and quality of Mackay's coal and fireclay, the free brickclay and the free use of his stone quarry and lime kilns, the Parys Mine Company set up its smelting works beside the Canal at Ravenhead. Contemporaries estimated that 700 tons of coal were used each week and the 10,000 tons of copper ore brought annually to Ravenhead yielded over 1,300 tons of copper. Most was taken to the company's Holywell works to be rolled or slit. Some left Ravenhead in small bars for the East Indies, and some as copper nails—invaluable in attaching copper sheathing to the hulls of sea-going ships. Other copper products, often bound for the African slave trade, were going down the Blackbrook branch of the canal from the Stanley copper works, founded in 1772, situated between the *Ship Inn* (then the *Sloop*) and Carr Mill.

Houses, such as Welsh Row at Ravenhead and the cottages that became Tontine Street, were built to accommodate both the workmen, needed and attracted by the new enterprises, and their families. A cotton mill was set up near Spray's Bridge; there was a foundry; the canal had graving docks and boatyards. Breweries, such as Greenall's in Hall Lane, Hardshaw, were busy. At Kitt's Bridge in the *Navigation Tavern*, the copper workers gathered socially. Their works manager, Joseph Harris, lived next door, where John Wesley preached on his first visit to 'St Helens, a small but populous town ... The people seem to be quite ripe for the Gospel'.

Opportunities for worship did exist. Quakers had met near the *Raven Inn* since 1679. In 1710 the Independents had built their 'New Chapel' not very far from St Helens Chapel, itself rebuilt after 1750. In September 1793, soon after legislation permitted Catholics to build churches, Mass was first said at St Mary's, Lowe House. The Methodists were able, in 1815, to move into their brand new Tontine Street chapel. By then Independents, Anglicans, Methodists and Catholics had an additional rôle: they had all established Sunday Schools where eager scholars (over 1,200 by 1819) were learning to read.

More privileged young ladies were pupils at the expensive boarding schools established at Parr Hall and Eccleston Hall. There were many smaller private schools charging parents a few pence weekly. As a result of bequests 30 children were attending Cowley School in College Lane, and 40 children the Anglican school, built, like its neighbour the workhouse, in Moorflat in 1793.

Although the St Helens of 1825 was to Baines 'a well built thriving town', it numbered only about 5,000 persons. These largely lived in the district of Hardshaw, at the south-east corner of Windle township, whose brook was one of the many twisting water-courses that had given boundaries to the four townships of Sutton, Windle, Eccleston and Parr, within which St Helens was developing.

The townships themselves still belonged to the ancient sprawling parish of Prescot, whose church and town lay three miles to the west, along the turnpike. Travellers by stage-coach to East Lancashire and to Yorkshire might come this way. Those journeying south would have had to take the other branch of the turnpike at Prescot and leave Lancashire by crossing the Mersey at Warrington.

Gradually coming downhill from Prescot, the turnpike travellers stayed in Eccleston township until, having descended Greenbank and crossed the boundary brook at Kitts Bridge into Bridge Street, they entered Windle. Small houses and shops flanked them until a 'T' junction took them with a right turn into Church Street. A glance to the left at this point would have shown them some small dwellings, the century-old Independent Chapel, the outline of the workhouse some distance away and then, as they looked north to Cowley Hill and beyond towards Moss Bank, all would be rural.

Premises of grocers, butchers, combmakers and coopers, inns and druggists' shops mingled with private residences to line Church Street. The 18th-century church had been enlarged in 1816—signifying an expanding population, but oddly was then re-dedicated to St Mary. (In 1926 the successor to the 18th century church was itself re-dedicated to St Helen.)

Beside the church lay Market Street—the market area with stone slabs for displaying wares sometimes so congested with vendors and shoppers that turnpike traffic was impeded. Further on, as the road became Raven Street, the aroma from Greenall's brewery might have occasioned a leftwards look for its source and the eye be taken by the more distant vista of Hardshaw Hall, its nearby windmill and, again, open countryside beyond. Quickly the *Raven Inn* would be reached, horses changed, refreshment sought. A three-storey building this, all in brick and contrasting sharply with its neighbour, the plain stone, mullioned, farmhouse-like Quaker Meeting House with its garden and burial ground.

Moving on again the travellers might halt abruptly as a swing bridge on the Sankey Canal closed against them and a barge (or 'flat') sailed past or was pulled on its way by men or horses. As the coach, now in Parr, journeyed on and roadside housing petered out, the headstocks and spoil heaps of many small collieries would become familiar sights, dotted amongst the fields and farmsteads.

What of Sutton, the fourth township, lying almost entirely south of the canal? The huge, smoke-emitting casting hall of the British Cast Plate Glass Company would have caught our travellers' attention before they reached Greenbank, as would the canalside works near Kitts Bridge. As they headed toward Ashton they would have seen the lane leading south through Sutton, climbing towards Peasley Cross and thence into open country, beyond which was the Prescot-Warrington turnpike.

Could our travellers, alert perhaps to the increasing importance of Liverpool and Manchester as port and textile centre respectively, and to a transport innovation at Darlington, have suspected that much was also about to change for the 'well-built thriving town' they had just left?

As Lancashire's workforce expanded, mills, factories and homes needed glazing. Where better than St Helens, with its coal, canal and easily available raw materials, to set up a company to manufacture crown glass? Good clay was present for making the crucibles in which the ingredients gradually fused in the heat generated by the coal-fired furnace. The 'mix' mainly needed sand. The British Cast Plate Glass Company had had their 'white' sand sent by water from King's Lynn. But windblown from south Lancashire's early coast line, and extending south-east into Windle, lay Shirdley Hill sand. It was close to the surface and of acceptable quality for most glass-making. Soda-ash, long obtained by burning kelp or barilla, was already being artificially produced, as salt-cake, from salt in Liverpool, and would shortly be made in St Helens. Limestone could be brought in by canal.

The rectangular site purchased for the St Helens Crown Glass Company lay on Grove Street just south of the canal, and glass was first made there in February 1827. Two of the company's partners were Peter Greenall (whose interest in the town came to extend far beyond his family's brewery), and his brother-in-law, William Pilkington, who, with his elder brother Richard, was then running the family's wine and spirit business, initially founded as a side-line by their doctor father. Three years later events had made Peter, William and Richard the sole shareholders in the glass company, by then 'Greenall and Pilkingtons', and eventually to become 'Pilkington Brothers'. While Richard Pilkington would cope with matters in St Helens, William was to seek business for the firm nationwide. Initially journeying by stage-coach, he could travel by railway train as the network developed, though not, as things turned out, with ease from St Helens itself.

Had it won Parliament's approval, the route originally proposed for a railway between Liverpool and Manchester would have run through Eccleston, having skirted on their north the Croxteth and Knowsley estates of the Earls of Sefton and Derby. Though Dr. Pilkington might have found it too close a neighbour when he retired to Windle Hall, the collieries at Cowley Hill, Gerards Bridge and Blackbrook would have been well served by this route, which after reaching Newton-le-Willows would have proceeded to Manchester in a very similar direction to the line opened in 1830.

How differently might St Helens have developed had not opposition from the canal companies and the two earls caused the Bill to fail. To have had a station directly situated on the nation's first fully fledged railway would have been significant for progress. As it was, the route selected for the Liverpool-Manchester Railway all but bypassed St Helens, entering Sutton from Rainhill and slanting north-east towards Newton-le-Willows.

Nevertheless, part of this stretch made railway history since between Rainhill and Lea Green stations (the line was by then in Sutton) the track was level; in October 1829 the famous Rainhill Trials were held there to determine if any steam locomotives were sufficiently powerful and reliable for use on the new railway. Forty trips to and fro had to be made. The winner, Robert Stephenson's 'Rocket', averaged 16 m.p.h. (allowing for the forty stops), and on occasion reached 30 m.p.h. With its load 'Rocket' also successfully climbed the line's inclined plane at Whiston, rendering the projected stationary engine there unnecessary, and ensuring that the railway was to be loco-motive-powered.

The changed course of Mill Lane at Marshall's Cross, caused by the building of the railway, shows clearly on Sutton maps. Close to the *Bull and Dog* and now bypassed, the original bridge over the line remains. So, too, does that in New Street (Workhouse Lane when the bridge was built, for Sutton's old workhouse stood immediately to the south-east). Beyond here the track ran down the Sutton Incline to what was to become St Helens Junction, on to Collins Green and across the viaduct to Newton, en route to its terminus at Liverpool Road, Manchester.

Aware of the increasing demand for coal, the distance of some local pits from the canal and the potential of rail transport, St Helens' coal owners and business men quickly subscribed £120,000 towards a railway to link the town with the Mersey. In May 1830, three months before the Liverpool and Manchester Railway opened, Royal Assent was given to the bill for the constructing of the St Helens and Runcorn Gap Railway.

This line was intended to serve Cowley Hill and Sutton collieries by conveying coal to a specially constructed dock connected by lock to the Mersey. The siting of St Helens' first station between the canal and Peasley Cross Lane showed passenger traffic to have been a secondary consideration.

Solving one of the line's many problems produced a famous railway landmark, the Intersection Bridge off Leach Lane, built to take Merseyside's second railway, the St Helens and Runcorn Gap, over its first, the Liverpool and Manchester. The scheme outran the capacity of existing locomotives and a stationary steam engine was provided to haul loaded wagons up the incline to the bridge.

An 1833 print shows the bridge in use. That July the dock was operating too. So also was the canal's new extension from Fidlers Ferry, with twin locks linking it to the Mersey just beside the Railway Dock.

Back in Sutton, St Helens Junction had been born when, in January 1832, a curve of track linked the completed St Helens section to the Liverpool-Manchester line, and thereby also enclosed the area of land which later became known as the 'Pudding Bag'. Initially a privately-owned horse-drawn carriage conveyed passengers between St Helens' first station and the Junction—a part of Sutton the railways had begun completely to transform.

One industrialist, James Muspratt, rapidly seized the chance to have both rail and canal transport available. To establish himself in Newton-le-Willows, where the 'Mucky Mountains' are still evidence of his alkali-making, he soon quit the works on land that he and Josias Christopher Gamble had leased at Gerards Bridge in 1828. Gamble, however, stayed put, manufacturing soda for Merseyside's expanding soap industry and for the glass makers, using salt and limestone brought by canal, and local coal. Sadly, the process also gave off hydrochloric acid. For better or worse, the chemical industry was now established in St Helens.

The community was mushrooming, but without co-ordination. More works were opening; jobs were plentiful, skilled wages high. People poured in, the population between 1830 and 1845 doubling to just under 11,800. Lodging houses were crammed, and new dwellings hastily thrown up for speculating landlords. Often one-up and one-down, some of these houses formed close-packed streets near established work places, as on Greenbank; others straggled along the main highways or clustered about new works—such as the rail complex at Sutton Oak.

It was best to live in Hardshaw to enjoy street lighting, piped water and paved streets, and to be connected to the only sewer (which discharged into the Hardshaw brook!). The other three townships, and the rest of Windle, each separately, and less progressively, attempted to solve the problems of urbanisation.

Hardshaw's progress (at the core of the town-to-be) was due mainly to its wealthy, energetic and public-spirited resident, Peter Greenall, the brewer. He backed the private Gas Light Company set up in 1832; he was chairman of the St Helens and Runcorn Gap Railway; having since 1824 provided water from the brewery supply, he ensured the creation of the St Helens Waterworks Company in 1843. When local provision for policing and magistrates was sought, the outcome, in 1839, was a grand, much-needed and multi-functional Town Hall. Of the original £3,000 subscribed, Peter Greenall (treasurer of the fund) contributed £300.

St Helens was spreading piecemeal over the large hollow within which the four townships converged. Peter Greenall realised both the necessity for providing an effective sanitation system, and the impossibility of doing so while the five authorities functioned independently.

Despite local opposition, he used his position as M.P. for Wigan (St Helens, then only part of the County District of South Lancashire, could not have its own M.P.) to secure the passing, in July 1845, of an 'Act for paving, lighting, cleansing, watering and otherwise improving the town of St Helens ... and for establishing and regulating a market therein'.

The Improvement Commission created by this Act should have brought effective local government into St Helens, but there were two immediate setbacks. Although the urbanised areas of Eccleston, Windle and Parr were included, pressure from its Cast Plate and Crown Glassworks had secured Sutton township's total exclusion from the Act. Within two months, the whole town was in mourning; tragically Peter Greenall, aged only 49, had died from a stroke.

He had led from the front, and, although for the next 17 years three of his henchmen—Samuel Bishop II (flint glass maker), Arthur Sinclair (Secretary of the St Helens and Runcorn Gap Railway) and David Gamble (proprietor of the Gerards Bridge Chemical works)—chaired the Commission, all too often its actions were dilatory and minimal.

Cholera had to strike twice, in 1849 and 1854, before the mile-long open sewer which the Hardshaw Brook had become was at least brick-bottomed. (It took typhoid for this to be replaced by a proper sewer in 1895!)

The Commissioners were not always to blame. Their funds were meagre—only £1,500 from rates in their first year. The much-needed Market Hall took only eleven months to build; it had taken five years to buy the site from the Quakers. Delay in completing the Rivington-Liverpool aqueduct frustrated plans to obtain water from it. Instead a shaft and pumping station had to be set up at Eccleston Hill.

Appropriately the Commissioners' Office was in Peter Greenall's Town Hall. Already containing the magistrates' court, police cells and the constable's house, it was also to house the Mechanics' Institute and St Helens' first public library. It could be hired for public meetings (Cobden spoke there in 1844), concerts, bazaars and elegant assemblies.

The Town Hall was situated at the centre of a busy expanding community. A stone's throw away, Tontine Street, in 1851, had 696 residents. Over half had been born outside the townships; many, though township-born, had at least one 'incomer' parent. Of the 91 heads of households, a third had local origins and a third came from elsewhere in Lancashire. Sixteen were from Ireland—it was five years since the Great Famine.

As existing industries grew they encouraged others. Ropes were made for canal and colliery haulage, and bricks to line pit shafts and build houses. Iron and brass coming to Daglish's huge canalside foundry might leave as locomotive, bridge, or even a new bell for St Mary's Church.

Local industries consumed an estimated 400,000 tons of coal in 1846. The previous year 440,000 tons had left the townships by canal and 252,877 tons by rail. Coal haulage was temptingly lucrative and in 1845 the canal proprietors agreed to merge with the St Helens and Runcorn Gap Railway Company. All too briefly, this new company was chaired by Peter Greenall.

Sadly for the canal, it did not receive the lion's share of the monopoly income of the new company. Alkali from the works was seeping into the watercourses that topped up the canal. When hydrochloric acid was poured in as well, the waters of the brooks bubbled, becoming noxious and corrosive. At Parr Mill the water wheel rotted away. Along the canal, coping stones were eroded and, like the masonry of the locks, needed constant repair. Yet the canal remained busy.

How did the railway develop? The track was improved and the inclined planes in Sutton made less steep, making the stationary engine unnecessary. To avoid tidal constraints and silting at the Railway Dock the line was extended to Garston, when a six-acre dock, complete with Daglish high speed coal drops, was built. Additional collieries were linked to the network.

At St Helens, railway passengers gradually fared better. The line was taken across the canal by a swing bridge to terminate at Salisbury Street (built opposite the Friends Meeting House). The first train left there in December 1849. Nine years later the Cricket Club had lost its pitch behind Raven Street when the Company leased land there (from the Sarah Cowley Trustees), and the line had been taken under a new bridge in Raven Street to a modest new station in Shaw Street. From here passengers could now travel to Rainford and thence to Southport, as well as, via Warrington, to Stockport. Salisbury Street remained in use for goods traffic.

One greedy move by the flourishing canal and railway company changed St Helens' future. Rail freight charges were doubled; canal rates (limited by law) grew only by half. Twelve tons of ingredients produced only one ton of soda. The resultant waste heaps, the 'chemics', were joining colliery tips as part of the landscape. Manufacturers realised that it would be more economical to move the coal to meet the salt. Thus, where canal and railway reached the Mersey, the Widnes chemical industry was born.

There was no immediate exodus by St Helens alkali makers. Established businesses expanded, but at what cost? As Lord Derby told the House of Lords: 'In the direction in which the wind ordinarily blew ... hardly a living tree was to be seen'. Legislation came: 95 per cent of all hydrochloric acid had to be condensed. Of little commercial value, three quarters of this went into the brooks.

Chemical and copper workers' lungs, teeth and skin suffered from direct exposure to chemicals and gases. Few made old bones. Frequently Irish, taking what work they could, they and their families lived close to the works, constantly inhaling, and ceasing to notice, their noxious vapours.

Thanks to one concerned chemical manufacturer, Andrew Kurtz, part of a house on Marshalls Cross Road, once home for the Gamble family, was leased from and renovated by Michael Hughes of Sherdley Hall. Kurtz equipped it. Thus, in January

1873, St Helens' first hospital—with nine beds—opened its doors. Soon Kurtz bought the entire house and three acres of land. These he gave to the Mayor and Corporation of St Helens (for in 1868 St Helens had achieved borough status).

All Sutton and Parr lay within the boundary of the new municipality, and much of Eccleston and Windle townships, where building had spread well beyond the boundary of the last (1851) Improvement Act—hence 'Newtown' as a district name. Under half of the 45,000 inhabitants of the new borough had lived within the area of the Improvement Commission.

Working hours were long, but jobs plentiful—at least for men. Young unmarried women, as census returns show, frequently sought work elsewhere, in service or in the cotton mills, some returning, when cheap transport became available, for brief week-end visits.

The smoky, smelly atmosphere had driven the elegant boarding schools elsewhere, but by 1870 so many denominational day schools had been set up that St Helens was unusual in having no need for a School Board. Clergy of all persuasions ensured adequate provision for their flocks, and they published statistics showing Board School education to be dearer than sectarian!

Sarah Cowley's small bequest of 1714 'for the bringing up of poore persons children to the scools at St Elens' depended on the income from her six-acre estate which lay beyond and behind the Friends Meeting House. Trustees administered the bequest. With Henry Berry and Sarah Clayton among the trustees, the canal was cut through the estate. Besides yielding £2 10s. 5d. annually, the cut revealed coal, by the early 19th century a source of far greater income. Benefiting still further when land from the estate was leased (at £550 per annum) to the St Helens Canal and Railway Company, the trustees were able to build a boys' school, 'Lacey's', towards the bottom of North Road.

Other schools frequently preceded or quickly followed the provision of new churches, as in Sutton (St Nicholas' and St Anne's), Parr (Holy Trinity and St Joseph's), Eccleston (Sacred Heart and St Thomas') and Windle (Holy Cross).

Mining and the furnace-based industries created great thirst, to be slaked at the town's many public houses and beershops. Pubs were meeting places too, for clubs and friendly societies. When local companies of the national defence force (the Volunteers) were set up, and their Mill Street headquarters provided by David (now Lt. Col.) Gamble, their namesake, the *Volunteer*, and the *Rifle Corps*, both nearby in Duke Street, must have been attractive after arduous drills.

Twice a year the fair came, and each June there was an exodus to Newton Races. From 1862 audiences could delight at performances in the newly-built Theatre Royal in Milk Street. Often lasting three days, fund-raising bazaars were popular social events especially if, after 1876, held in the Borough's splendid new Town Hall.

Houses for the more prosperous began to spread into St Ann's, West Park, Eccleston Park, and along Cowley Hill Lane. Terraced streets continued to multiply, but for everyone pleasant countryside lay within walking distance. Annual works outings took people further afield, and 1871 saw the opening of a replacement railway station in Shaw Street. This also provided direct services to Wigan and to Huyton—no need now to go to Liverpool via St Helens Junction.

Passengers had a choice of local newspapers to read. In these, local advertisements and coverage of national events preceded St Helens' news, which included almost word-for-word accounts of meetings, however acrimonious, of the Borough Council and its committees. Sporting activities were reported—the first rugby team included members of well-known local families. Weddings and funerals of the town's élite were described in minute detail. Accounts of court cases (from 1882 the Borough had its own bench) dwelt on more sordid matters.

One advertisement became world-famous. Thomas Beecham had initially sold his home-made pills by post or in the market as 'worth a guinea a box', and when, in 1887, he and his son Joseph opened their handsome factory in Westfield Street, the slogan was to be seen carved into the face of the building.

The St Helens of which Joseph Beecham became mayor in November 1899 had changed considerably since its incorporation in 1868. The Borough now had its own M.P. and, with extended boundaries, had in 1889 become a County Borough. There were 83,000 inhabitants. Not only was the corporation supplying gas: it had also embarked on providing electricity, to the use of which its tramways were being converted.

However belated the council had been in building a sewer to replace the foul open brook, it could congratulate itself on pioneering a depot to supply sterilised humanised milk for infants. The isolation hospital, too, was municipally-run, set up because neither voluntary hospital (the Providence had opened in 1882) accepted patients with infectious diseases.

The town now had two splendid parks and an incipient museum. David Gamble had recently funded a combined technical school and public library building, and Sarah Cowley's trustees had erected two imposing middle schools in Cowley Hill Lane.

Coal-mining and glass-making (bottles as well as flat glass) provided most employment. The brickyards, tile works and foundries were busy—but one major industry was in decline. All the local alkali-makers used the Leblanc process to decompose salt, and in 1890, when threatened by rival processes, they combined with other Leblanc producers to sell out to, and become shareholders in, the United Alkali Company. Financial survival was crucial for the new company and costs were thought to be lower in its Widnes works. The chemical industry gradually abandoned St Helens.

Whereas distant dreaming spires might signal Oxford's presence, tall crowding chimneys, pit heaps and 'chemics', a pall of smoke and mellow, echoing factory hooters (released from wartime silence on 3 April 1945) would identify St Helens long into the 20th century.

Not so now. Enlarged, in 1974, and created a Metropolitan Borough, St Helens today includes Haydock, Newton-le-Willows and Earlestown, Rainford, Bold, part of Billinge and the remainder of Eccleston and Windle townships. Industrial employment has shrunk. Mines and waste heaps have gone. In a far 'greener' town it is largely the churches of St Helens' original townships that form the landmarks.

Early Days

1 In 1435 Sir Thomas Gerard of Bryn founded a chantry at Windleshaw whose priest would 'celebrate for the souls of the founder's antecessors for ever'. After the Reformation the chapel and old cross to its south (similar to those at Peasley Cross and Marshall's Cross) fell into decay. Later, possibly in 1627, the date on the cross's shaft, the land within and around Windleshaw 'Abbey' became a Catholic burial ground, as this early 19th-century lithograph by J. Bell shows. Mrs. Elizabeth Lowe, mother of the foundress of Lowe House Church, and de la Bruyère, the French glassmaker, are interred here.

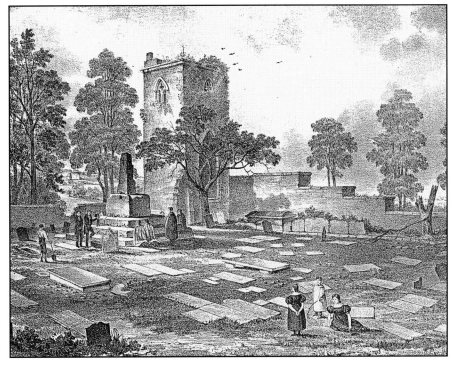

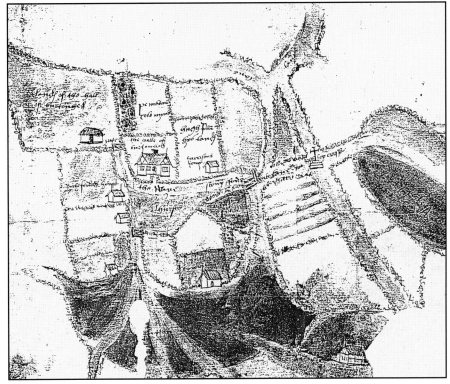

2 In the Scarisbrick papers at the Lancashire Record Office is the original of the *c.*1580 plan of the Burtonhead estate. It includes sketches of more distant churches but not St Elyn's chapel, a mile away. The estate lay in Sutton, mainly to the west of Peasley Cross, which shows clearly. Largest of the buildings is long-vanished Burtonhead Hall. Dark blotches on the plot behind this are significant. They are the pits of 'Pemb[er]tons Cole Myne'— dug in an area where seams outcropped or lay close to the surface.

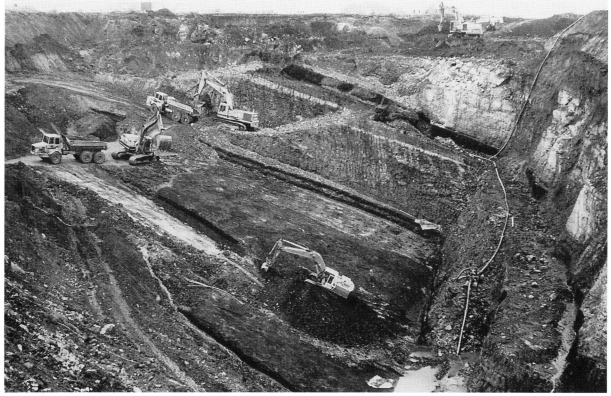

3 Very recent reclamation of industrially polluted land both between Canal Street and Borough Road and from behind Burtonhead Road to beyond the new Linkway (East) created gigantic chasms which provided dramatic evidence of coal-mining since the 16th century.

Coal seams dipping to the east show clearly in this view of the huge excavators at work. Uppermost are remains of 17th- and 18th-century pillar and stall workings in Potato Delph (seam). Below, being stripped by open-cast operations, is the multi-layered Earthy Delph. On the skyline Pilkington's Prescot Road office tower is just visible.

Elsewhere in the Potato Delph workings a line of silver birch pit props was uncovered. Positioned at the centre of the coal being worked, they are thought to date from the late 1500s and indicate deeper and more sophisticated mining than was carried out not so far away at Pemb[er]ton's.

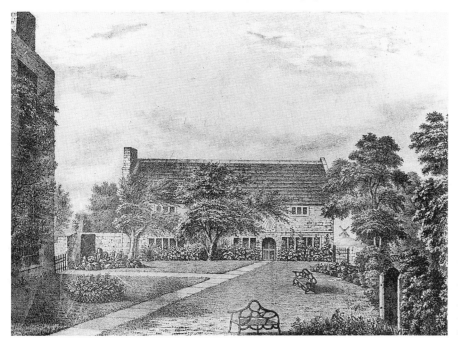

4 This engraving, with the *Raven Inn* on the left, and Hardshaw Mill background right, centres on a Hardshaw building, with its 1753 sundial.

It had been standing long before 1679 when, as shown by court records of fines imposed and furnishings seized, Quakers were meeting there. Registered for Quaker worship in 1689, the Friends Meeting House, with other local land, was in 1694 bequeathed in trust to Hardshaw Monthly Meeting. George Shaw of Bickerstaffe, donor of these 10¾ local (almost 23 statute) acres, is commemorated in nearby street names. Presbyterians used the building 1863-8 until their Tolver Street church was completed.

5 Parr's coal was not being exploited when William Clayton, Liverpool merchant, M.P. and ex-mayor, bought the Parr Hall estate in 1713. It was his daughter Sarah, to whom it passed in 1745, who grasped the opportunity provided by the cutting of the Sankey Navigation 10 years later. Pits were sunk and coals ready for sale even before the new waterway reached her estate. Her wealth, common sense and assurance show in this portrait by Joseph Wright of Derby. Significant in developing the St Helens coalfield, she has at her fingertips the plan of her Liverpool creation, Clayton Square.

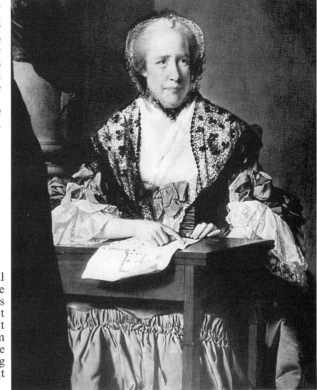

6 Ravenhead's development into a major Industrial Revolution location became obvious with the construction of the British Cast Plate Glass Company's manufactory in 1773. Then the country's largest industrial building (113yds. long by 50 wide), the great casting hall with its arches might at first glance seem cathedral-like within. Externally its size and the smoke issuing from its orifices, together with the wall separating the complex from the surrounding countryside, made it much more menacing.

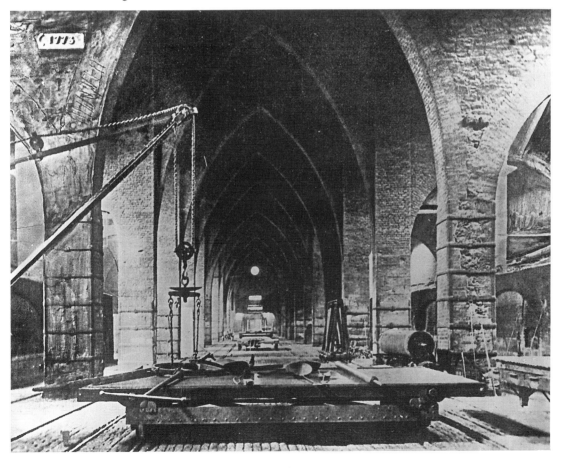

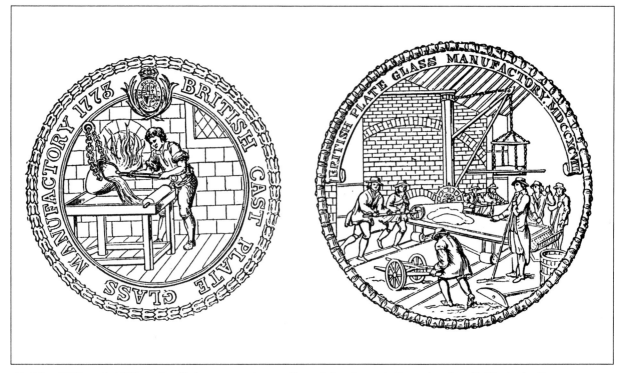

7 The 1773 and 1798 seals of the companies casting plate glass at Ravenhead well illustrate the processes involved. Illustration [8] shows a similar group at a casting table. Is it likewise mounted on rollers enabling it to be moved along the hall from furnace to furnace?

In 1901 the Ravenhead works were bought by Pilkington. For a while glass rough cast there was finished at Cowley Hill. Subsequently the hall was subdivided. With part used as a store, it—like many other notable St Helens buildings—caught fire, and in May 1974 the town lost a significant part of its industrial heritage.

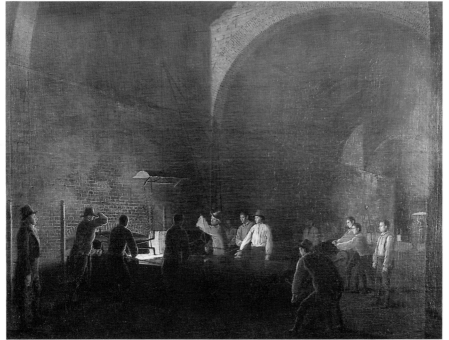

8 Although French crafts-men (who added 'pontil', 'marver', 'parison' and 'cullet' to glassmakers' vocabulary) were brought in, glassmaking at Ravenhead was far from perfect until Robert Sherbourne became manager in 1792. Improvements, such as adding cullet (waste glass) to the mix and using covered crucibles to keep soot from the melting ingredients, raised quality and profits.

In the painting, after Joseph Wright of Derby, at Pilkington Glass Museum, Sherbourne stands at the extreme left watching molten glass being poured onto a casting table in Ravenhead's great casting hall.

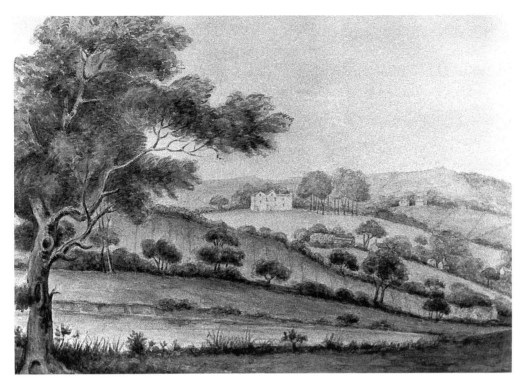

9 Robert Sherbourne himself painted several local scenes, which reveal how emptily rural the area then was. 'Cowley House and Billinge Beacon', which he painted in 1793, is now with other watercolours of his at Manchester Central Library. This 1962 copy, by A.T. Free, suggests Sherbourne's vantage point was overlooking the turnpike near Cropper's Hill, not far from his Ravenhead works.

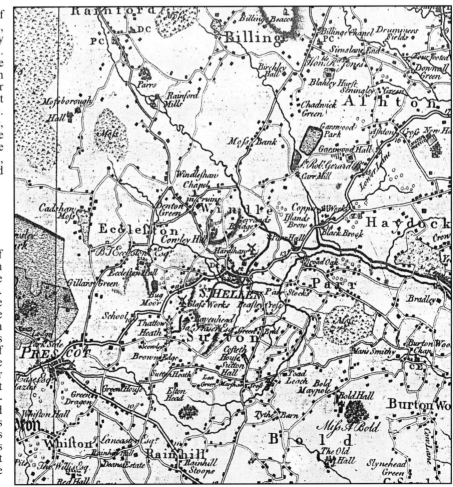

10 William Yates's map of Lancashire was published in 1786, about six years after the fieldwork was completed. Accurately surveyed (Billinge Beacon and Prescot Spire were two of the triangulation stations used), it shows, in this section, the 'St Hellen' of c.1780. Familiar roads are marked, together with water courses, canal, coal pits at 'Thattow' Heath, the glassworks, and several wind and water mills. Larger residences are named, and sometimes their owners. Other dwellings are scattered thinly, apart from those lining the future Church Street.

In 'Naylor's Tenement'

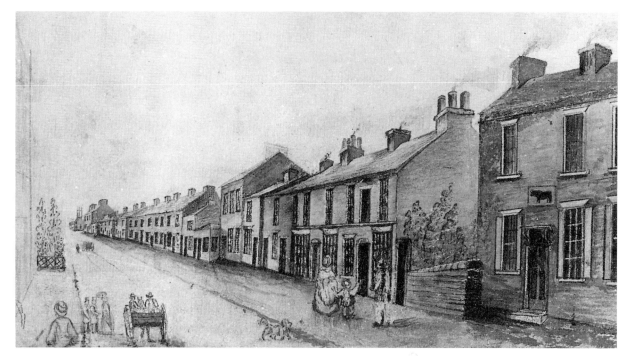

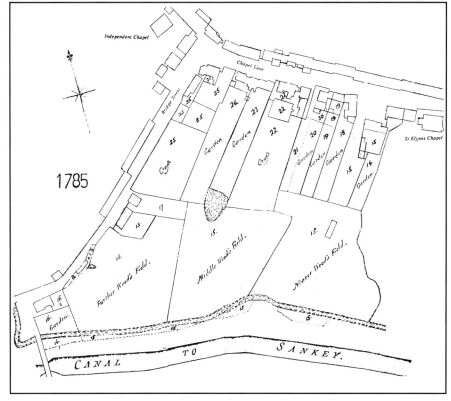

11 In this 1805 sketch by John Knowles of Chapel Lane (later Church Street) from the *Black Bull* on the right to St Helens Chapel (the future Parish Church) in the distance, the inn and houses formed one boundary of a block of Quaker-owned land called Naylor's Tenement.

12 This version of a 1785 plan (the numbers refer to a schedule of leases) shows Naylor's Tenement as yet undeveloped. Gardens and then fields reached from the Chapel Lane houses to the (Hardshaw) brook and the Sankey Canal. Yet, bounded by Bridge Street, Church Street and what became Market Street and reaching almost to the canal, the tenement was to become the core of the town, containing Tontine Street, the first Town Hall, the markets, the County Court and Naylor Street itself.

13 In April 1815 the first public service was held in the new Methodist chapel in Tontine Street, successor to the one erected in Market Street in 1801. Quietly brick built, it could seat 450 and had its own graveyard. At one point dwindling numbers led to the building's being divided into six cottages, but expansion came, particularly with a revival in the 1860s. This culminated in a new church being built in Cotham (now Corporation) Street in 1869. (Just over a century later, beset by dry rot and its own vastness, this was demolished and Wesley House erected in its stead.) Thereafter the Tontine Street building became a mission chapel, until it was sold to St Helens Corporation in 1890 for £1,000 and subsequently demolished as part of an improvement scheme. Burials had ceased in 1858. Rumour claims that a leaden coffin was found years later when foundations were laid for the *Nelson Hotel* beyond the confines of the graveyard.

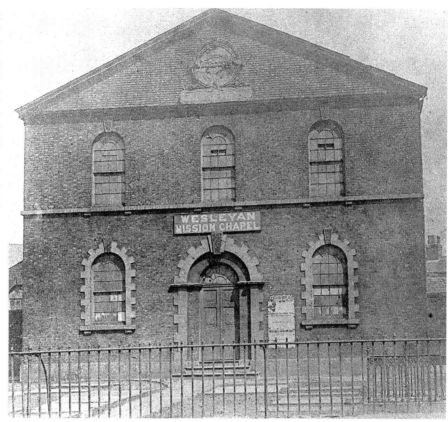

14 Here a delivery boy on his over-large bicycle is heading from Liverpool Road into Tontine Street, soon to be demolished; a coal cart approaches. Far behind it is the telephone exchange with the *Robin Hood Inn* close to it. In 1851 the inn had 21 residents—the carter/beerseller and his family, one servant and 14 lodgers. Sir James Sexton, M.P. for St Helens 1918-31, once lived at number 18, where his parents were umbrella makers.

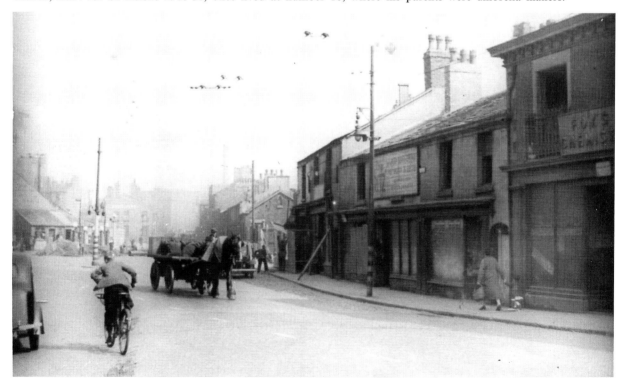

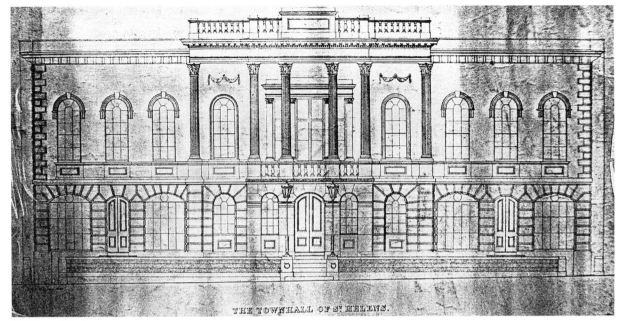

THE TOWN HALL OF ST HELENS.

15 This imposing building, erected by public subscription, on the west side of the New Market Place, was opened on 8 October 1839. Peter Greenall had been the prime mover, and that day in its assembly room (whose court room furnishings were designed to vanish below floor level), his wife entertained the invited guests to luncheon. The Town Hall became the venue for social events, from a cavalry ball given by Sir John Gerard, to concerts and public meetings. In addition to the courtroom there were rooms for the magistrates, a bridewell and a house for the constable. The Improvement Commissioners met here. It housed the Mechanics Institute, and found space for the first public library. Much used, it was partly burned down in 1871 (luckily Gallie's wines, stored in the basement, escaped the conflagration), repaired, and caught fire a second time in July 1873. It was decided to erect another building—more suited to the growing town with its new status of borough.

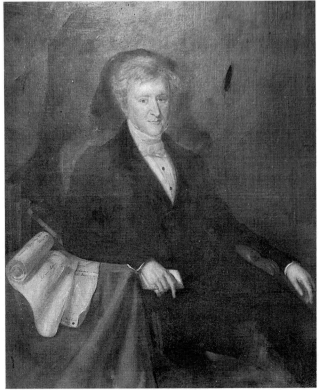

16 Peter Greenall's portrait first hung in the old Town Hall, whose construction he had promoted. Painted in 1845, by Spindler, it was paid for by public subscription in recognition of Peter Greenall's rôle in the creation of the Improvement Commission, the petition for which is rolled at his right elbow. Unexpectedly he died before the completion of the portrait, which now hangs in the Town Hall Council Chamber.

17 James Brockbank, chronicler of local events writing in 1896, termed this edifice 'the municipal buildings'. Bearing 'closed' notices and with windows broken, it stands awaiting demolition to make way for the Covered Market of 1889. Where its long Exchange Street frontage ended, butchers' shambles, their iron columns re-cycled from the former market sheds, extended to Bridge Street. It is not yet known when or by whom the building was erected. Nothing stood on this site beside the Town Hall on the 60in. 1849 O.S. map. Some copies of this photograph caption it 'Butchers' shambles and council offices'.

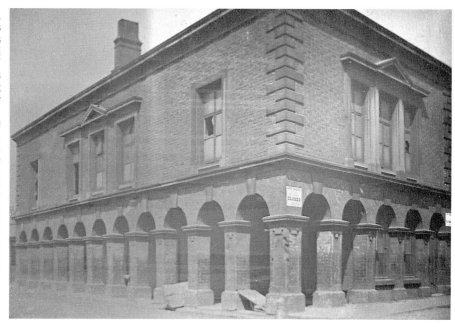

18 When the first Town Hall was demolished after 1876 temporary market stalls quickly filled the vacant site. More permanent stalls were to be found in the 1851 Market Hall, built by George Harris, just visible in the background.

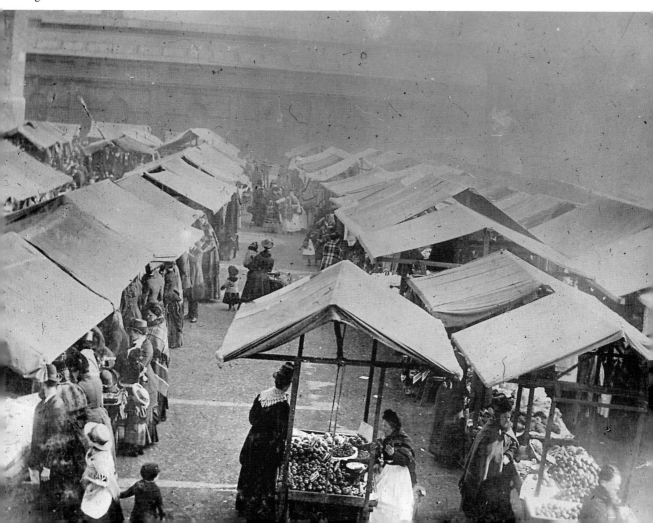

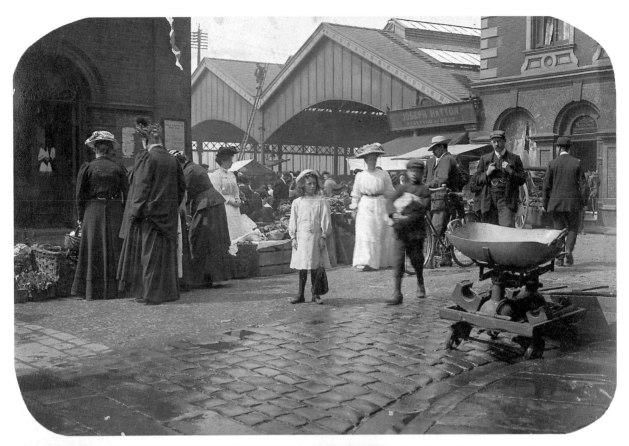

19 Demolition of the 'municipal buildings' [17] followed and in 1888-9 the Covered Market was built, extending back to Bridge Street and across to Exchange Street. Trading continued to take place in the roadway between the Market Hall (top left) and the Covered Market (background centre), seen here in Edwardian times, until the whole area was swallowed by the 'Church Square' re-development of the 1970s.

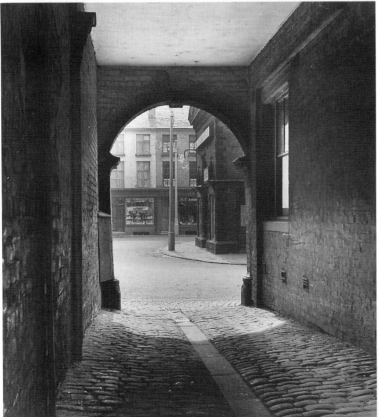

20 Photographed in the 1950s in Sunday quiet and from within Victoria Passage (to the right of the Victoria Hotel beside the Covered Market) is the Naylor Street North end of the Market Hall. Beyond it are the once elegant houses of the New Market Place, their ground floors converted into shops.

Along the Towpath

21 Canal craft were usually too familiar and ordinary to photograph. Fortunately, in 1901, this scene was captured by someone standing north of the canal, near Parr Hall (once owned by Sarah Clayton), and looking towards the embankment that carried the railway from St Helens Central Station to Haydock. What was happening? The flat was stationary with a gangplank to the bank, which seems to have crumbled. Were repairs underway and the cart's load ready to plug the gap?

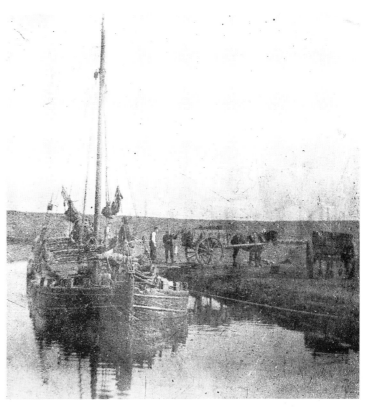

22 In this 1901 scene the photographer was looking towards the canal's Gerard's Bridge terminus. Beyond, to the right of St Mark's spire, the chimneys belong to Pilkington's plate glass works at Cowley Hill. 'Burgy', waste sand and rouge used in grinding and polishing and piped from the works, has yet to form the banks that will rise to hide the railway on the right.

Craft for the Ravenhead branch of the canal would turn left here before ascending the New Double Lock, aided by the bollard just visible beyond the fence.

Across the branch are the Globe Alkali Works of the United Alkali Company. Here, set in open country with collieries at hand and the canal to bring salt and to take their products away, James Muspratt and Josias Gamble built the town's first alkali works.

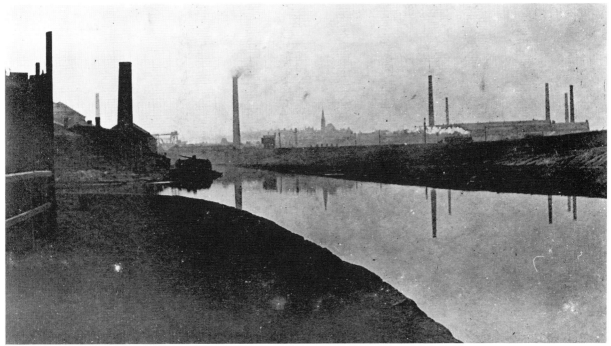

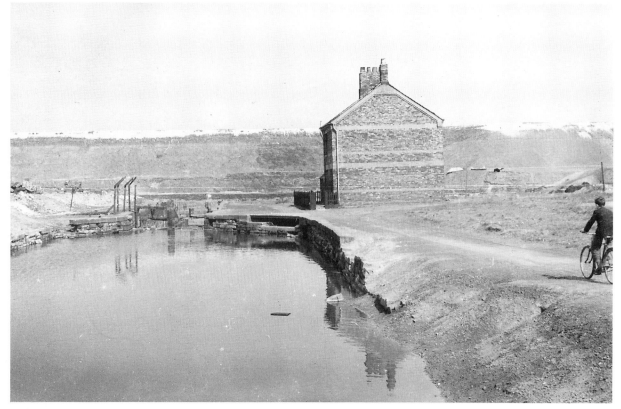

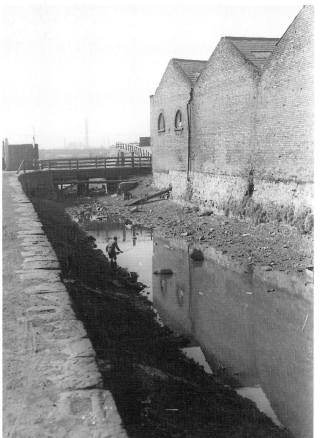

23 Opened in 1770, the New Double Lock, with two chambers and three sets of gates, gave access to the section of canal that terminated at the far end of present-day Canal Street, and had a branch leading towards Burtonhead. Flats using the lock could wait in the basin in the foreground. Like the other locks, the double lock had its keeper's cottage, which overlooked the canal T-junction. By the 1950s burgy from the glass works had formed the high terraced bank beyond the lock, its top bright with newly deposited sand and rouge.

The cottage has been lost but, fortunately, the upper gates, jammed by mounting debris in the lock chamber, long survived the closure of the canal. They were replaced when the restoration of the lock and basin was completed in 1993.

24 Here, seen in 1955, stand the warehouses of Forster's Glass Company—later to become Rockware—but the stone courses below the brickwork date from the Union Plate Glass Company, whose site Forster's took over. Prominent on the left are the coping stones, some grooved by ropes as the canal craft were manoeuvred. Rectangular depressions reveal their previous use as railway sleeper blocks, the two holes drilled in each showing where the chair to hold the rail had been attached. The swing bridge crossing the canal links Pocket Nook Street and Standish Street—now a rather straighter road. In the distance, the Corporation Street bridge spans canal and railway.

25 By 1805 the *Ship Inn* stood beside the narrow swing bridge carrying the road to Parr and Peasley Cross. Streets spread beyond it, and, re-fronted and extended, it survived until 1934. Urbanisation had also brought a wider road, with its stone setts, an iron bridge (with wood block roadway), and trams, which with all other traffic had to halt when the bridge was raised. On the post to the right of the lattice work can be seen the wheel used to operate the bridge, which was itself replaced in 1937 and the canal culverted beneath it.

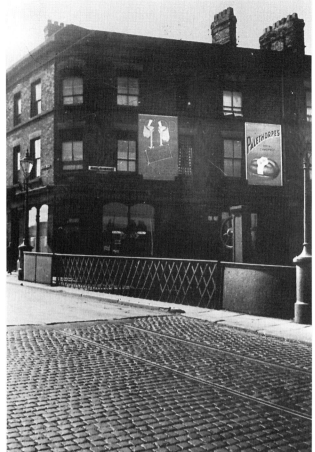

26 Beyond the signal box, railway track and stonemason's yard, the canal is invisible, until, centre right, the short branch leading into the huge complex of Kurtz's Sutton Alkali Works can be detected. Here, two flats are revealed by their masts and rigging, moored one each side, rudders to the camera.

The alkali works had expanded enormously from the canal-side site which Andrew George Kurtz inherited from his father in 1846. Well before this picture was taken in the mid-1890s and they formed part of the United Alkali Company, the works extended beyond Warrington New Road to Langtree (now Jackson) Street.

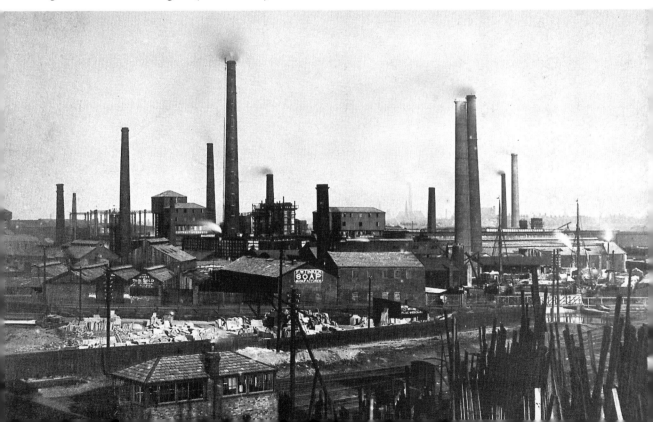

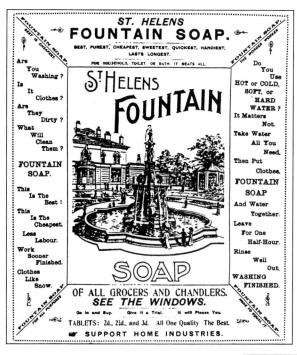

27 Soap-making was never an important St Helens industry. Instead, soda went from the town to the major soaperies beside the Mersey. However, from 1852, F.W. Tinker made soap at his canalside works—which show clearly at the centre of illustration [26]. It was he and his wife who, in 1888, gave a new pulpit to the Parish Church, placed so that all could see the preacher, and he who laid one of the Y.M.C.A.'s foundation stones.

The firm's 'Fountain Soap' advertisement, of 1903, features, rather larger-than-life, the handsome terracotta fountain presented by Sir Henry Doulton, and much admired since its installation in the formal garden of Victoria Park.

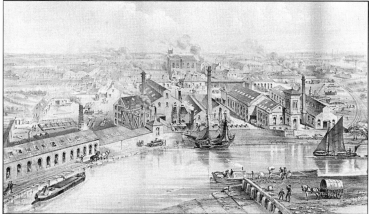

28 This lithograph from Waterlow and Sons of about 1860 shows St Helens Foundry. Run by Robert Daglish in succession to his father, the foundry's products ranged from colliery winding engines to bridges erected as far afield as Dublin and Calcutta. Materials reached and produce left the foundry by the canal. A barge drawn by two horses can be seen in the foreground. One flat is moored at the foundry, another sails up towards the Ravenhead (Canal Street) terminus of the canal. Smoke billows across the small but crowded town in which the Parish Church is, apart from the foundry complex, the most prominent building.

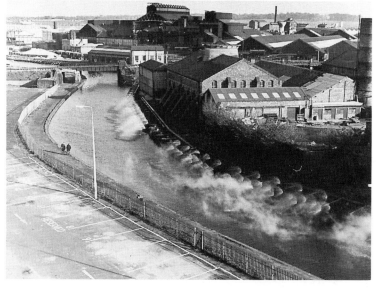

29 In 1970, industry crowds the south bank of the canal. Daglish's foundry has given way to a car park; sections of wall to the left of the St Helens-Liverpool railway bridge are its only remains. Clouds of steam form as water used in the glassworks for cooling is discharged boiling hot into the canal. These are the 'Hotties'. Beyond them the protruding cone, however truncated, connects the buttressed brick building with glassmaking. Designed by John Taylor, a church architect, it had been built in 1887. The cone acted as a great chimney over the then innovatory tank below, which, constantly fed with raw materials, made continuous production of blown cylinder glass possible.

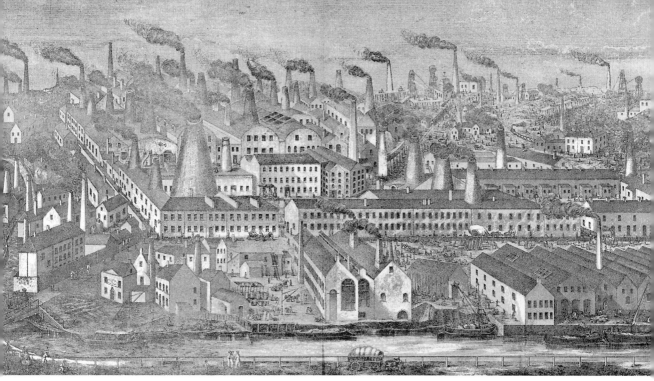

30 In this 1868 artist's impression of Pilkington's Glassworks, Collieries and Brickworks (as seen from Greenbank), the town lies away to the left. The continuous row of buildings parallel to the canal is on Grove Street. The terrace to the right and that behind it form Pilkington Row, built to house incoming workers and their families. The 1826 St Helens Crown Glass Works' cone looms largest and nearest: collieries and brickworks appear background right. The Tavern Bridge (bottom left) will turn for the various canal craft to pass. To its right stands the *Navigation Tavern* once frequented by the copper workers.

31 Here, in 1898, a solitary figure walks the canal towpath and is close to where three people stood talking in the illustration above. The protective railings remain but the canal has been drained and its bank shored up. It is about to be filled in. Having erected offices in Grove Street, Pilkington will soon extend further and build over the canal bed, so that present-day Canal Street really follows the line of the towpath. Then brand new, the 1897 Jubilee Clock and tower will eventually have to make way for the 1930s Head Office complex.

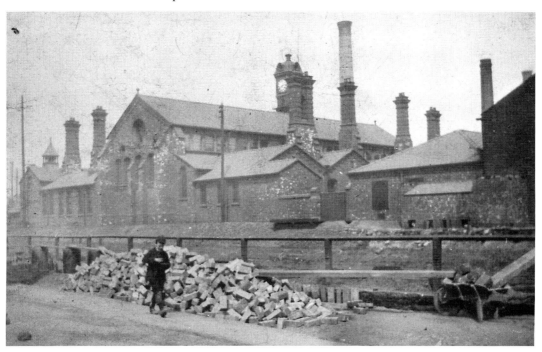

Using the Railway

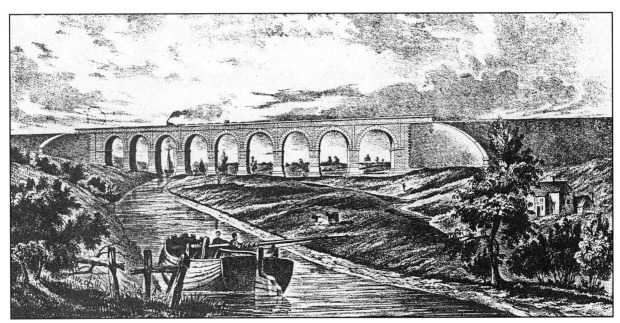

32 Outside the four townships, but since 1974 within the Metropolitan Borough boundary, is the site where in 1830 England's first fully-fledged railway, the Liverpool-Manchester, crossed the first industrial canal, the Sankey. In this lithograph, by W. Benson of St Helens, the Sankey Brook meanders to the right of the canal. In the foreground, its mast lowered, a 'flat' with its large long-tillered rudder is motionless. Another approaches through the viaduct, whose 60-ft. tall arch gives just sufficient clearance. Immediately overhead a train steams towards Manchester.

33 Opened in 1833 to transport St Helens coal to the Mersey, the infant St Helens and Runcorn Gap Railway is seen in this Bury-Ackermann print. In Sutton, a locomotive of the 'Novelty' type is crossing the Liverpool and Manchester Railway by the two-span Intersection Bridge, hauling coal wagons to the company's Widnes dock. Below, heading towards Manchester, is a 'Rocket' type locomotive; to its right Leach Lane becomes Penlake Lane beyond the bridge—a rural scene doomed to obliteration as the railways prospered, prompting and prompted by industrial expansion.

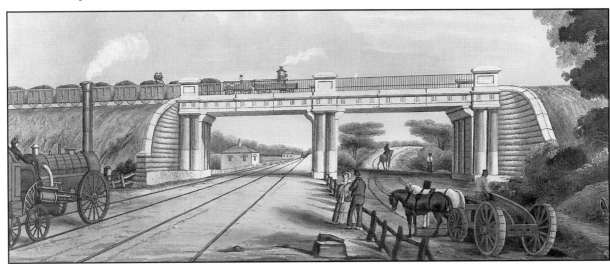

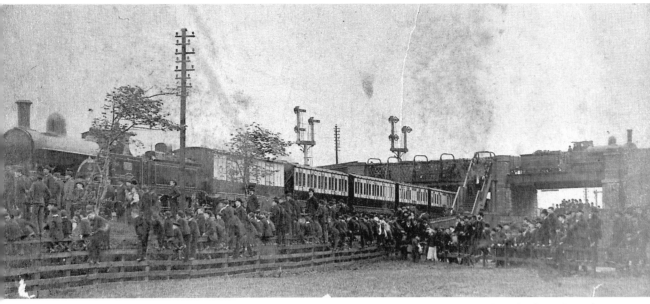

34 Widened and far less elegant, the Intersection Bridge is again being crossed by a goods train from St Helens in this late 19th-century photograph. Some pedestrians stand on the footbridge across the Liverpool-Manchester line, but precisely when and why the trackside crowd gathered is uncertain. Undoubtedly their attention is not on the stationary Liverpool-bound passenger train. One theory is that a royal train was imminent.

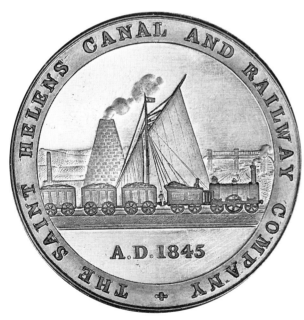

35 This seal marks the amalgamation in 1845 of the struggling St Helens and Runcorn Gap Railway with the prosperous Sankey Canal. The Intersection Bridge can be seen in the background; nearer lies a cone-shaped glass house; the sails are of a canal barge, or 'flat', heading towards St Helens. In the opposite direction a locomotive—looking more modern than 'Novelty' or 'Rocket'—hauls coal towards the Widnes dock. Streaming smoke and steam and well-filled sails suggest movement and progress appropriate to the town and to a go-ahead transport undertaking.

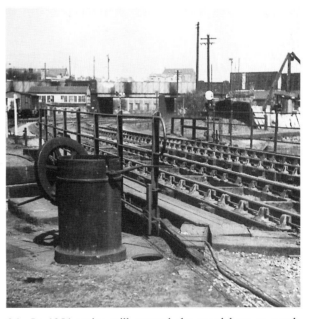

36 In 1954 trains still crossed the canal here to reach Shaw Street from St Helens Junction. This swing bridge was controlled from the signal box standing to the left of the stout iron-sided bridge, built in Raven Street (Church Street) when the St Helens Railway was extended to Rainford. Originally the sturdy mechanism in the foreground, with its handle and wheel, had been used to operate the bridge manually. The Hippodrome and Holy Cross Church protrude on to the skyline, and, to the right, sheerlegs pin-point Melling's stonemason's yard.

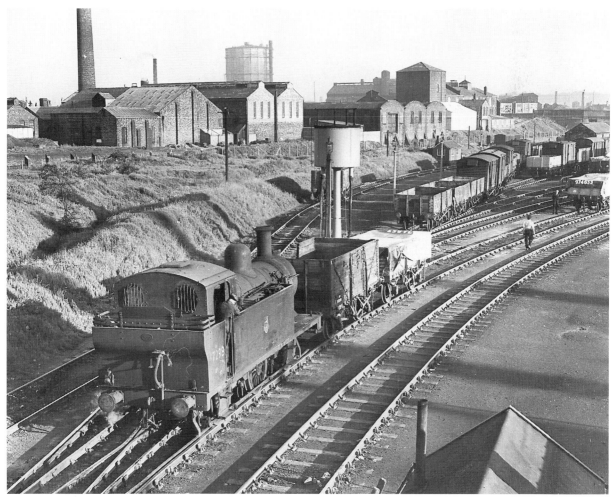

37 Known as 'Tintus', locomotive 47298, seen here when Shaw Street had a busy goods yard, is no ordinary tank shunter. Built in 1924, it reached Sutton Oak loco sheds in the early 1950s and worked throughout the area, until withdrawn from service in the mid-1960s and destined for scrap. In 1974 the Liverpool Locomotive Group rescued it. Back-breaking restoration followed until in 1980 LMS 7298 paraded and shunted faultlessly in the 'Rocket 150' celebrations. Still working well, it is now at Llangollen.

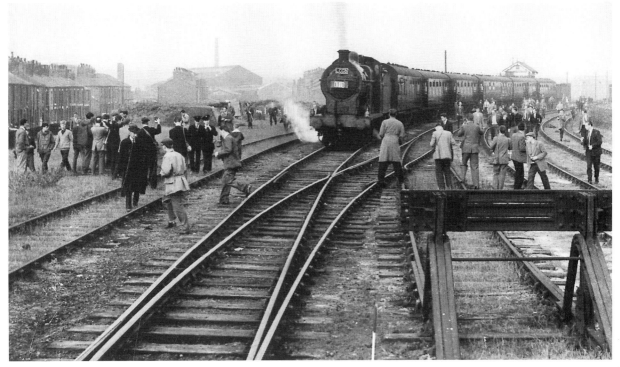

38 This was no ordinary train that was approaching the Central Station in 1961, long after its passenger services ceased. The freight locomotive with its L.M.S. rolling stock was taking members of the Locomotive Club of Great Britain on a rail tour along former freight lines before they vanished. The party had alighted temporarily and was being provided with a chance for photography.

39 In bad weather, to reach the carriage-length canopy's protection, Central Station's passengers had had to dash half the length of the platform. Here, after closure, canopy, platform and track stand derelict and, like Central Street to the left, would soon disappear. Passenger services to the station had ended on 3 March 1952 and goods on 4 January 1965.

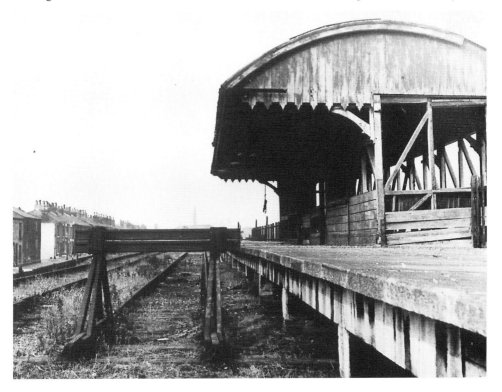

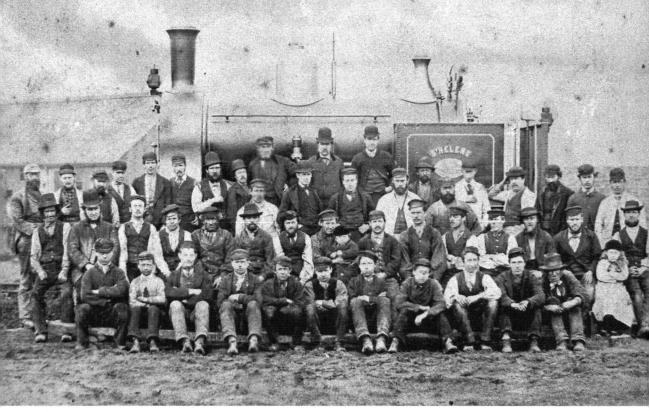

40 By 1871, Edward Borrows, former locomotive superintendent of the St Helens Canal and Railway Company, employed 26 men and seven boys in the Providence Foundry he had set up adjoining his Peckers Hill home. Borrows and Sons' locomotives were compact and robust for industrial use. With their water contained in a tank mounted below the boiler, they needed no tender. Augmented by two small children, the foundry workforce is here posing in front of the early and cabless *St Helens*, with Borrows' family members standing centre back.

41 St Helens firms using Borrows' locomotives included Pilkington. In this 1955 photograph *Briars Hey* approaches pulling three flat trucks, on the first of which large near-vertical sheets of glass are held secure.

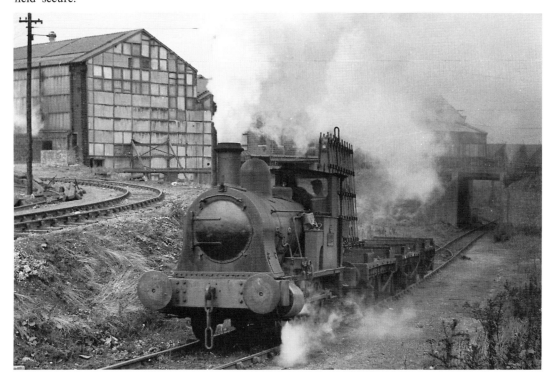

Owners and Occupiers

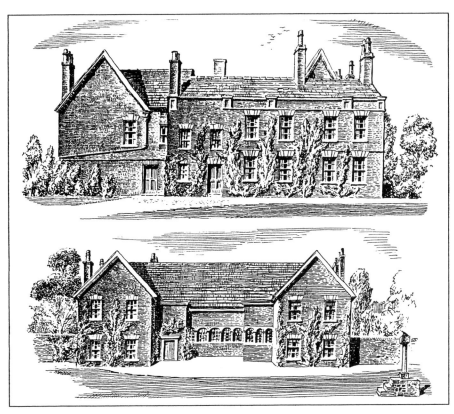

42 When, in 1820, Samuel Taylor, then 18, inherited the Eccleston Hall estate from his father, its 1812 purchaser, the hall was used as a boarding school. It had replaced a medieval building (whose post holes were discovered in 1991) and by 1664 could boast 24 hearths. Only its circular Elizabethan fish pond has survived, but fortunately this second hall was sketched before, in 1825, Samuel re-built it, married and took up residence.

The wide door and range of curve-topped windows, seen in the 'sundial' sketch, suggest that a single-storeyed hall, probably with projecting bays, was the nucleus of the second hall. The building's actual shape and size can only be guessed at, for the gables and chimneys of the two sketches neither tally nor connect.

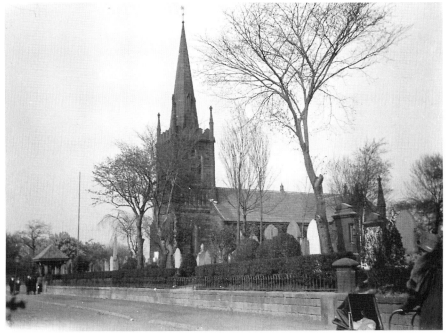

43 It was Samuel Taylor who both funded and ably designed Christ Church, Eccleston, seen here almost a century after its consecration in 1838. The splendid hammerbeam roof and pews are of oak, likewise the pulpit (allegedly carved by Grinling Gibbons) brought from St Saviour's, Southwark. In its leafy setting, Christ Church became a favoured venue for fashionable weddings and funerals. When St Peter's, Church Street, Liverpool, was demolished in 1922 its 1795 clock was given to Christ Church. The new dials needed were made at the Mill Brow foundry.

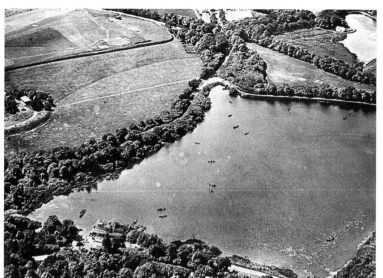

44 Taylor Park Lake was not created for the leisurely summer boating observed in this aerial photograph. The 'Big Dam' of the Eccleston estate, its purpose was to store water needed to operate the corn mill on Mill Brow. From 1844 with additional reservoirs—one the Leg of Mutton Dam (top right)—water was piped to form part of the town's supply.

Top centre are the chalets of Eccleston Hall Sanatorium; top left the bunkers identify Grange Park Golf Course, laid out here in 1923 to augment the club's original 9-hole course of 1891 behind the *Grange Park Hotel*. The straight path between the course and the park uses the inclined plane running down from the former sandstone quarry (later aviary), from whose stone Christ Church, Eccleston, was built.

45 When the Parys Mine Company set up its copper smelting works at Ravenhead in the 1780s Michael Hughes I, in charge of all their operations, came to live at The Tickles, which he re-named Sutton Lodge, near the works and the canal.

Through successive purchases he became Sutton's major landholder. He rose socially—J.P. in 1800 and a Deputy Lieutenant for Lancashire in 1806. By then he had built Sherdley House ('Hall') as his home, for which some furnishings travelled London-Liverpool by canal. The house is seen here, in snow, about 1880. It was demolished in 1949, after the Borough had acquired the estate, which has become Sherdley Park.

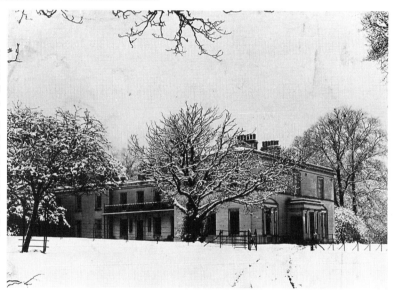

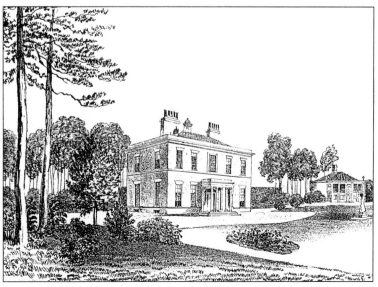

46 Nutgrove House (now Hall), Thatto Heath, was built in 1810 for Liverpool printer Jonas Nuttall and Frances his wife. Devout Methodists, their generosity ranged from providing Millbrook House, Eccleston, as a peaceful place where Adam Clarke, Methodist scholar and preacher, could complete his vast 'Commentary' to using their kitchen as an impromptu chapel.

Jonas' nephew Thomas, botanist and Harvard professor, had inherited when Shaw drew Nutgrove *c*.1850. Its grounds retain some of his plantings. The house passed next to Jonas' great-nephew Francis Dixon-Nuttall, the glass bottlemaker, and more recently served as an old persons' home.

47 'Ingleholme' was the Eccleston Park house that Frederick Dixon-Nuttall, son and business successor to Francis, bought and extended in 1909. Twice mayor, and an alderman until 1923, Frederick Dixon-Nuttall gave the Eccleston Lane Ends war memorial, unveiled in 1922, to commemorate all in West Derby hundred who fought and died in the Great War—as had one of his sons.

The family's days at 'Ingleholme' ended abruptly in April 1928 when fire destroyed its upper floor. Within a year Mr. and Mrs. Dixon-Nuttall were both dead. In 1934 'Ingleholme' began a new life as a hostel for Pilkington trainees.

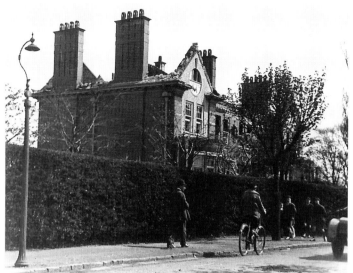

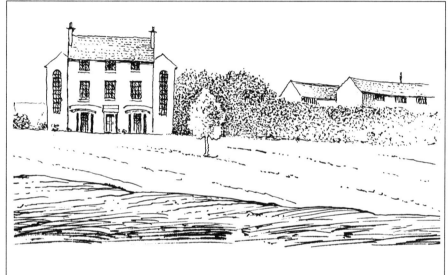

48 This recent interpretation of an indistinct contemporary sketch shows Windle Hall as it was when, in 1826, Sir John Gerard leased it at £300 a year to Dr. William Pilkington. He retired there from the wine and spirits business he had established in 1813, after 25 years as a surgeon apothecary. Initially from Horwich, he had been apprenticed to a Hardshaw doctor, William Fildes, to whose practice he and a colleague succeeded. Windle Hall remains a Pilkington family home, though its appearance has changed.

49 Haresfinch House was originally flat-fronted. Its porch and bay windows were added by colliery-owner David Bromilow, when the house was extended and much refurbished for his daughter and heiress Julia's grand wedding in 1862.

By 1873 David Bromilow had quit St Helens, and Haresfinch was the residence of St Helens' second mayor, Llewellyn W. Evans, when he married Caroline Kate Ansdell.

It passed into Gamble and Varley hands before the Corporation bought it in 1960. No longer walled, the grounds form an attractive park, but the house has vanished.

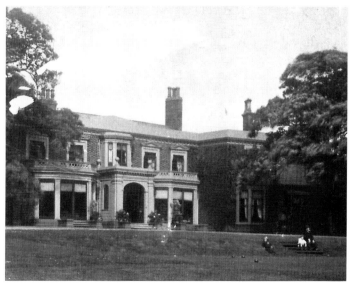

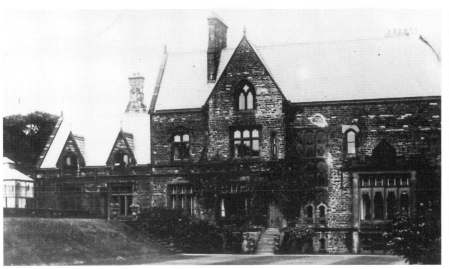

50 Photographs of 'Windle-hurst', the house built for David Gamble near Hard Lane and facing Cowley Hill, are rare. The Hard Lane entrance lodge survives. 'Windlehurst' was a sizeable Victorian mansion and from 1924-44 accommodated the headmaster and junior classes (for 8-11 year olds) of Cowley Boys' School.

When St Helens' first 'garden suburb' was laid out in the 1920s on former 'Windlehurst' land bordering Bishop Road, some roadways followed the paths of David Gamble's estate.

51 James Wilton McTear came to Sutton before 1871 to manage the Copper Rolling Mills, living at Milestone House (also called Roughdales Farm) in Chester Lane, opposite Four Acre Lane, where this family photograph was taken. Did any son help farm the eight acres there? McTear was a 'farmer' in the 1881 census, and when the family moved in 1894 it was 'St Michael's House and Farm' at Micklehead Green that he leased. A busy person, McTear also managed Roughdales brick and tile works which had by 1894 expanded almost to Milestone House. He served on St Helens Hospital Committee for its first 40 years and, from 1897, was a J.P. A Colonel, presumably in the Volunteers, from 1900, he and his family moved to Huyton in 1911 where he died five years later.

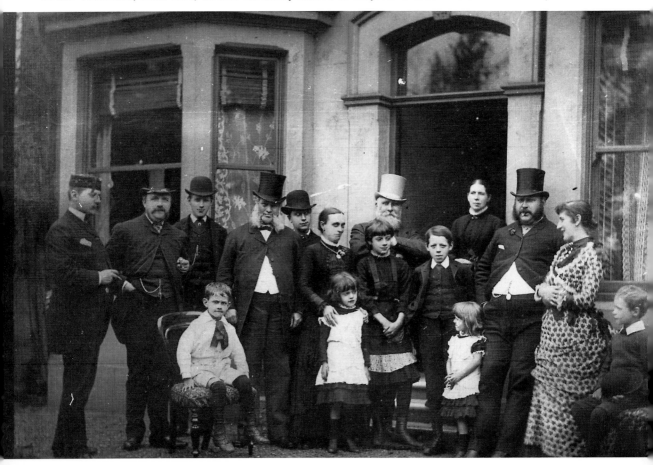

52 Sandfield Crescent, on Greenbank, was convex rather than concave. Seen here shortly before its demolition, it curves away towards Liverpool Road and the substantial 'Crescent House' (not in view), tenanted in 1847 by Arthur Sinclair. (Secretary to the canal and railway company, and Improvement Commissioner, Sinclair became mayor in 1892.)

Changes in doorways, door steps and chimneys reveal piecemeal development. The four houses on the left, their rear access via a central passageway, have two fireplaces apiece and lack the glass fanlights, double doorsteps (and higher floor-level) and sandstone plinths of the five-chimneyed houses nearer to those with the pediment at the centre of the Crescent.

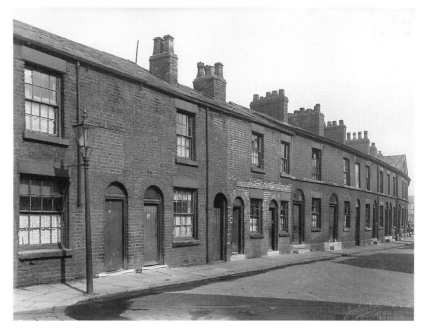

53 St Helens' then murky atmosphere is evident in this early 20th-century view of Milk Street, where washing hung across the cul-de-sac was becoming increasingly off-white. Just discernible on the left, beyond the Wesleyan School buildings and to the right of the gaslamp, are the two upper windows of No.13, Thomas Beecham's first St Helens home, where he made and marketed his highly successful pills.

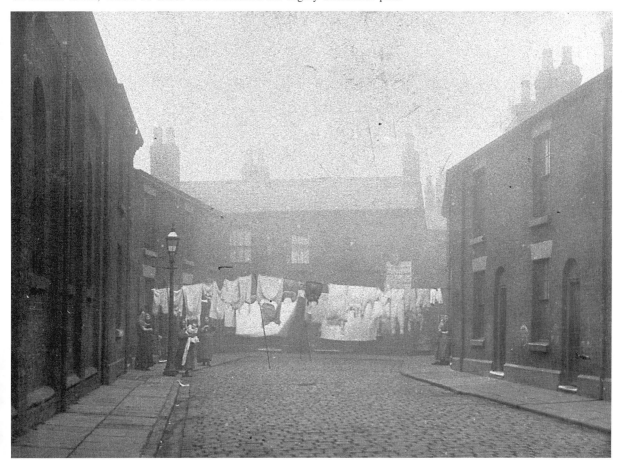

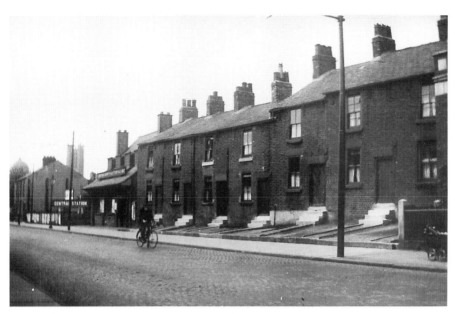

54 These houses, with their whitened steps, were the first to be built on the north side of Corporation Street. They featured on the 1888 O.S. map—when there was no Central Station. As late as this 1938 photograph, the street was still gas-lit and paved with granite setts. At the right, behind the sturdy pram, is a corner of the Mining School. To the left, the tower of Lowe House Church and the dome of the Y.M.C.A. are just visible in the distance.

55 Numbering by an unknown hand helps interpret this 1913 view from Beecham's clock tower. Top left '2' is the Gamble Institute. The Parish Church is '5', and '6' is Greenall's brewery. In front of this '1' marks the Congregational Sunday School rooms. Dark and to the left '7' are the Imperial Buildings (even now initialled A.D. for their builder, the grocer Alphonsus Dennett). '3' marks Brook Street, and '4' the then Salvation Army Citadel, in front of which, un-numbered, is the L-shaped Wesleyan school. White-washed back yards and bright lines of washing contrast with the smoke-darkened walls of the crowding houses and small workshops.

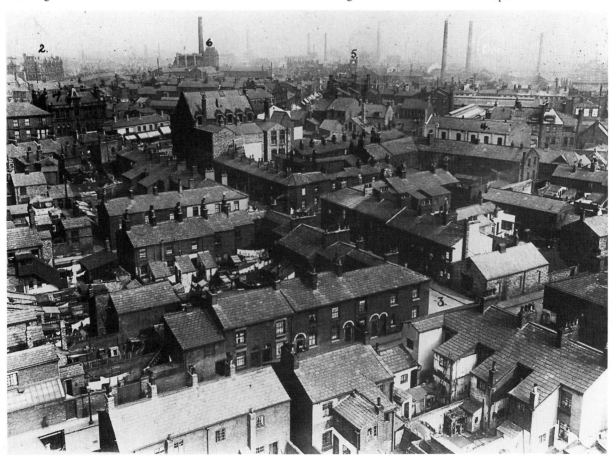

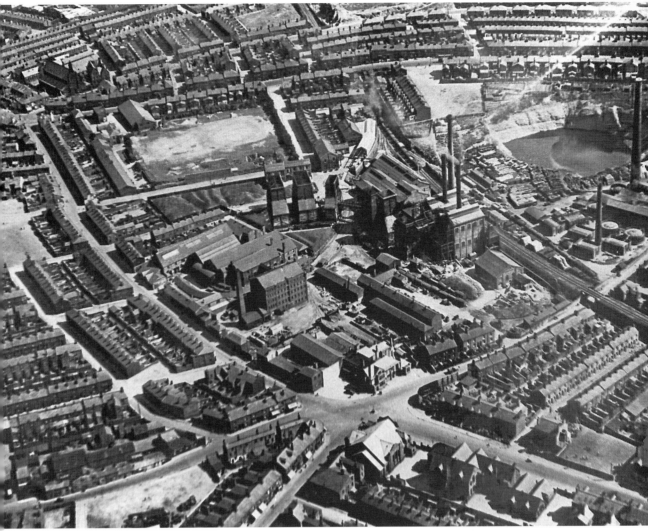

56 In this sunlit but treeless *c.*1930 photograph Boundary Road (marking the Improvement Commissioners'
boundary) curves upwards from left to right. Crossing it by a bridge is the railway that once ran to the right
beyond Triplex to Eccleston Hall Colliery. The track leads past the power station and its sidings to the tunnel
below Croppers Hill which a train is entering. Right of the track is Doulton's pottery, its huge waterlogged clayhole
nowadays a car park. At Fiveways the *Nag's Head*, United Reformed church and school show clearly. They remain
today, whereas Eccleston Street has lost its houses, the large Co-op bakery, and the carpet factory's chimney.

With the Glassmakers

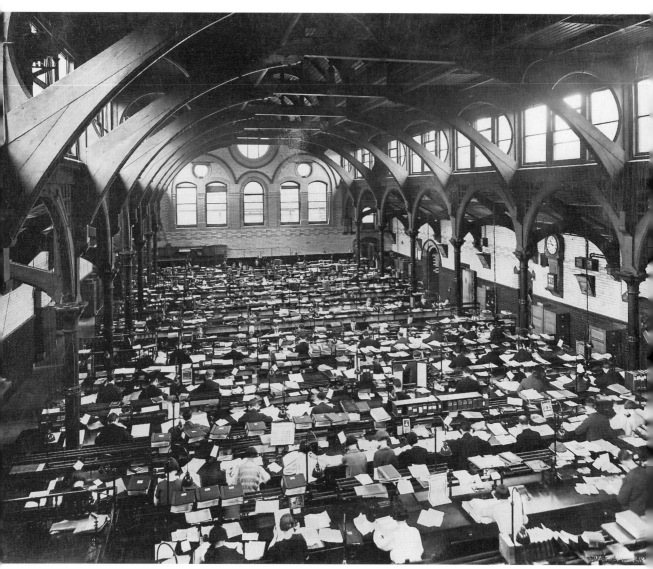

57 The three circular windows at the far end of Pilkington's vast general office at Grove Street identify it in the canal bank photograph [31]. Built in 1886, its sheer size and sturdy internal roof structure are impressive, as is the diligent concentration of its 1926 staff. In 1995 it survives an empty, threatened, listed building.

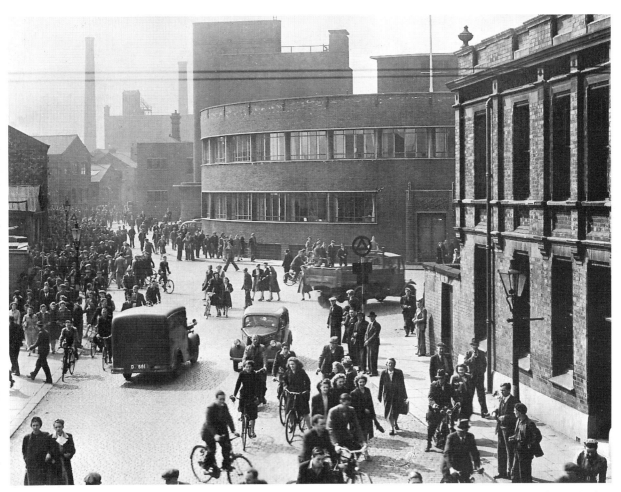

58 On this sunny late 1940s day Pilkington employees' dinner-time exodus almost fills Grove Street. Sheet Works are background left. The curved façade belongs to the combined Head Office/Canteen block designed by Herbert Rowse and completed in 1940. Using locally made hand-rubbed bricks, it extends and joins the earlier Canal Street and Grove Street buildings. All three are listed. Fortunately, only two vehicles are heading past the *Bridge Hotel* on the right towards Canal Street against the cyclists oblivious to the Highway Code.

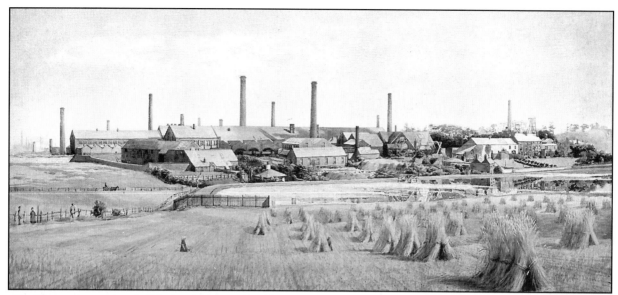

59 The great casting hall is hard to spot in this 1890 watercolour by John B. Gibbs of the much expanded Ravenhead Glassworks, as seen from Prescot Road. Partly occupying a former stone quarry the pool shows behind the stooked corn. Beyond this, on the skyline, is the headgear of Alexandra Colliery, named, as was Alexandra Drive, to mark the then Princess of Wales' visit to Ravenhead in November 1865. The painting formed part of the 1908 Summer Exhibition at the Mansion House.

60 By 1960 the former cornfield was a builders' quagmire as Pilkington's new Head Office took shape. Here the pool has been extended into a lake, and a 12-storey tower block, its windowless ends clad with dark blue glass, nears completion. So, too, does the low horizontal block in the centre of the picture, which will become the Glass Museum. Designed by Fry, Drew and Partners, the head office complex was fully completed in 1965.

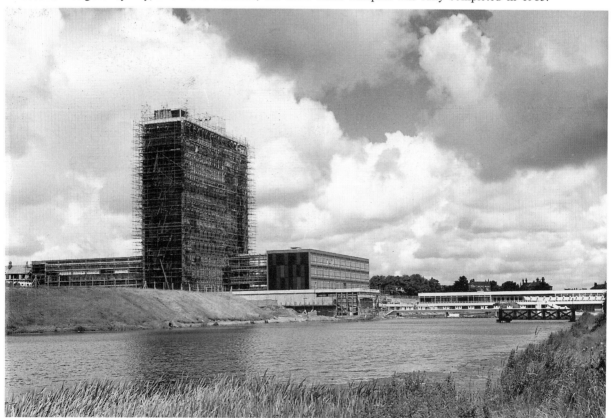

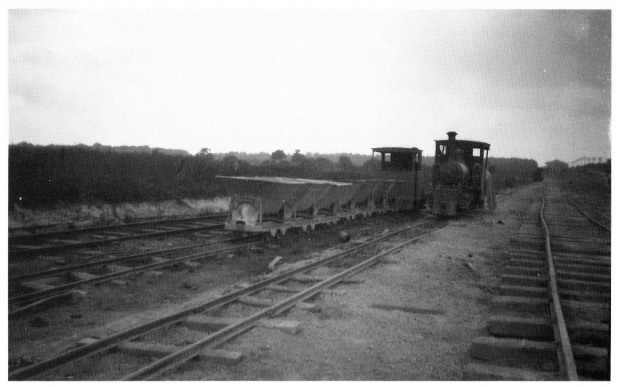

61 Sand, essential as a glassmaking ingredient, and also for grinding, lay beneath the topsoil of large areas northwest of St Helens. Sometimes 3-4ft. in depth, it was loaded into hoppers and taken along temporary narrow gauge track, as here, to the sandwash at Rainford, close beside the railway to St Helens. After the line closed sand reached the works by road until in 1977 operations at Rainford were run down. Successfully restored to agriculture, the former sand extraction sites only reveal themselves by their depth below the roadways with which they were once level.

62 The Union Plate Glass Company, their works built on Greenall land at Pocket Nook, began production in 1837. The unusually tall chimney in the centre of this 1854 illustration (from Bradshaw's *Handbook of the Manufacturing Districts of Great Britain*) suggests that the company was making, and not buying in, the saltcake it needed as an ingredient. The works expanded, having 540 employees by 1865, but intense foreign competition caused it to close in 1898. (Profits from sheet glass kept Pilkington going.)

By 1912 Forster and Sons had expanded from Atlas Street into the vacant works. No longer needed by Rockware, who took over Forster's at the beginning of 1968, the site was cleared and is now occupied by St Helens Technology Campus.

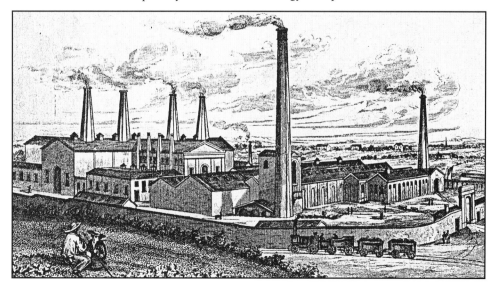

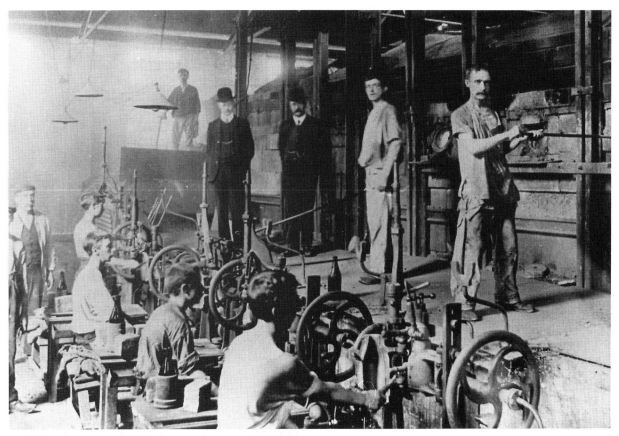

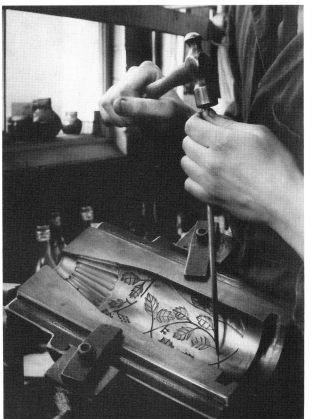

63 In 1900 bottles were being made on these Boucher semi-automatic machines, produced and then installed by their U.K. licencee, John Forster, at his Atlas Street engineering works, having been spurned by existing bottlemakers.

He stands (black-suited and moustached), beyond the machines near the specially-built tank from which glass was gathered, to be machine-blown with a mould. One stands open on the right-hand machine. John Forster served the town as councillor, mayor and alderman. His concerned chairmanship of the Health Committee gave St Helens the country's first infant milk depot in August 1899.

64 However streamlined and automatic glass bottlemaking could become, skilled craftsmen remained essential. These hands belong to a 1956 Forster's apprentice engaged in completing the engraving of an ornamental design on a bottle mould.

Ex Terra Lucem (et Argillam)

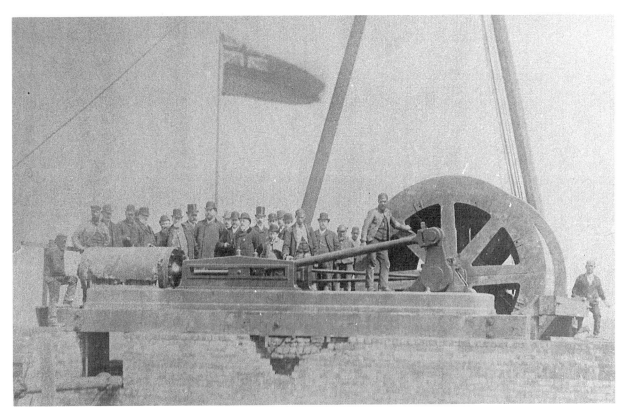

65 Despite the flag, the party assembled in the early 1890s for the opening of the Worsley Mesnes Colliery Company's Eccleston Hall Colliery were standing on dry land, behind one of the winding engines. The engine house had yet to be built. The company utilised two shafts from earlier workings, initially to drain water that had accumulated, and then to deepen them to 660ft. to reach the Rushy Park and Arley seams. The colliery had about 300 employees and used the branch railway built in 1859 to Gillars Green Colliery. It closed in 1910.

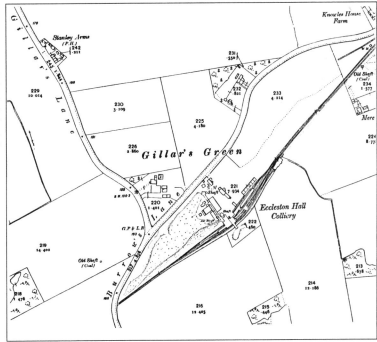

66 Eccleston Hall Colliery as shown on the 1908 25in. O.S. map (scale reduced).

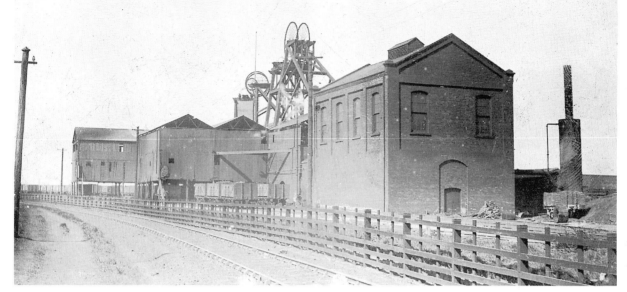

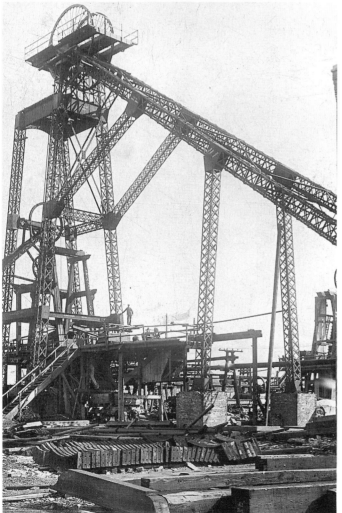

67 Parr No.4 pit, which together with Parr No.5 formed Richard Evans' Southport Colliery, also worked the Rushy Park seam. Sunk in 1894 between Newton Road and the canal, the colliery's surface buildings and the headgear to each shaft are seen here. A mineral railway passes below the left-hand building from which the screened (cleaned and graded) coal can be dropped into waiting wagons. At one time having 700 employees, the colliery was abandoned in 1936 after flooding.

68 Sutton Manor Colliery began life when the first shaft was sunk in 1906. It became, with closures, St Helens' last working colliery. Until the pit's recent closure, one of the oldest remaining steam winding engines in the country was still in operation for men and materials. All surface features of the colliery have been erased. This photograph shows the headgear operated from the steam winding engine.

69 Necessity prompted less formal coal-getting in the 1921 and 1926 strikes. Sunk near St George's Road, this pit penetrated workings abandoned long since—possibly even before the 1842 Mines Act, as a pair of corsets were found there. Whilst elsewhere in the town strikers' families might unofficially pick spoil heaps for domestic fuel, coal hauled to the surface (note the pulley and cord) at this West Park site is said to have departed clandestinely by road to Liverpool.

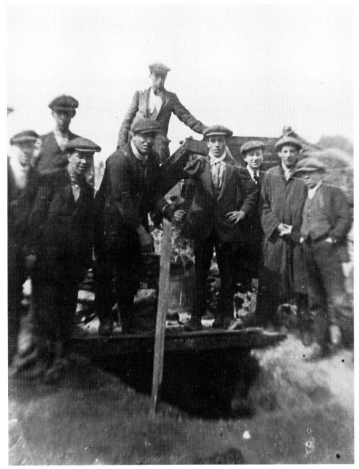

70 Ravenhead's richness in coal and clay, realised by Mackay in the 1770s, is revealed in this pre-1968 photograph of Burtonhead Road. A clayhole, with buildings at its bottom, lies in shadow in the left foreground. Beyond it the steep corner of another catches the sun. Ravenhead Brickworks' buildings are to the left, adjoining those of Ravenhead (previously Grove's) Colliery with the two headgears. Shafts 1,600ft. deep were sunk in 1866, and at the colliery's closure in 1968 its annual output was 207,000 tons.

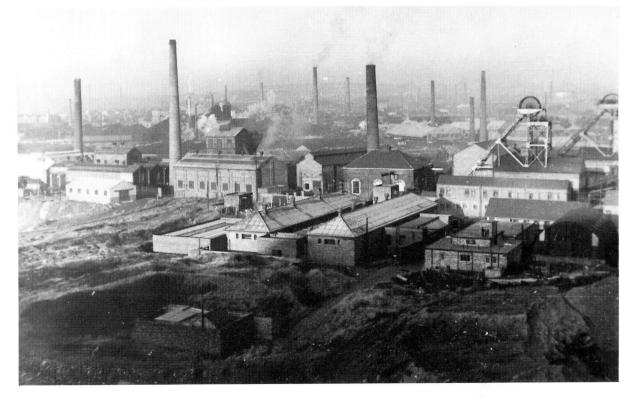

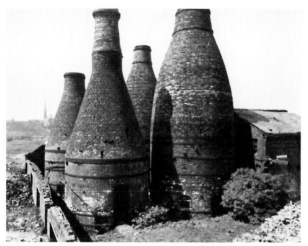

71 & 72 The Old Teapot Brickworks was close by, exploiting the same rich clay for its wares and coal for its furnaces, access to which was through the rectangular openings seen in the wall to the left. The works included a Hoffman Kiln, as well as these bottle-shaped kilns—quite different from glass cones. A small arched doorway at the base of each gave access for stacking the wares for firing.

73 That maps named the area south of Marshall's Cross and west of Chester Lane 'Roughdales' suggests early digging into its clay. By 1879 The Roughdales Fire Clay Company had established an extensive clay pit bordering Chester Lane. This 1890 photograph reveals the cycle of operations at Roughdales in J.W. McTear's [51] time. Clay, hauled up rails from the hole (bottom right), is pushed in tubs along the overhead track bridging the site and is prepared for the round-topped kilns. These and their chimneys stand at the left. Nearer the camera, beside the temporary railway line, bricks and sanitary pipeware await despatch.

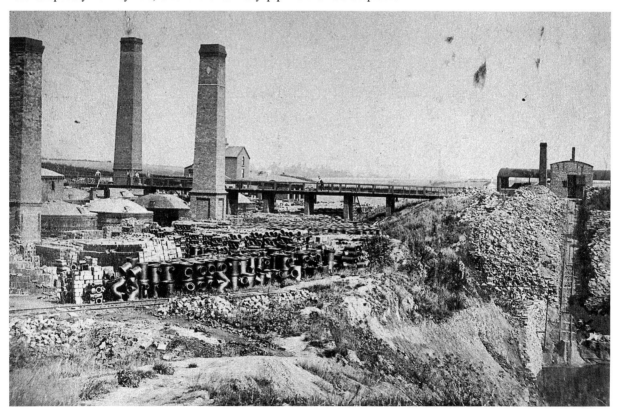

Beer and Chemicals

74 Beer from the Hall Street brewery established in 1762 by Thomas Greenall was increasingly needed as St Helens' thirst-promoting extractive and furnace industries expanded. For two centuries the brewery grew too, occupying much of the area now covered by the Hardshaw Centre. To the left, in 'Nat Tousin's' 1976 drawing, the building with the canopied hoist stored malt at ground level and grain above. Reaching the tower top by conveyor, the barley was gravity-screened before being sufficiently milled to crack the grains and aid sprouting. Power for the mill and heating for the coppers in the arch-windowed copper room came originally from steam engines on the floor below—hence the tall chimney.

75 Seen from Greenall's tower between the wars, the urban landscape merges into industrial haze. Bishop's glassworks' cone stands out. The gasworks' chimneys are to the right. Bottom left, its face to Hall Street, the substantial house with its wide chimney-stack was Peter Greenall's home, later becoming the gas company's offices and (1875-1908) the Conservative Club.

Peeping over Hall Street are the windows (centre right) of the coachmen's cottages above the coaching houses in Haydock Street. Swire's forge, built to make nails and clog irons, is at their right: the premises opposite with wide part-gabled roof were once Cammack's mineral water works. Greenall's bottling store occupies the right foreground.

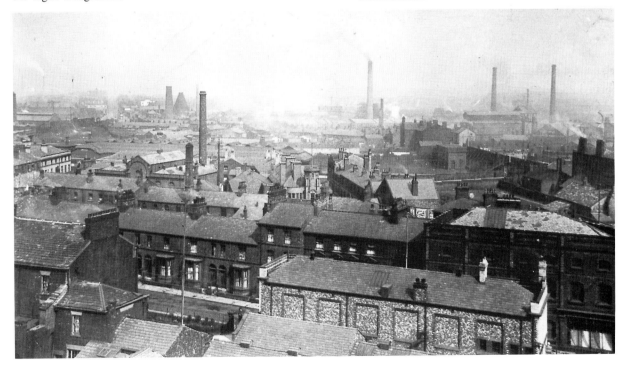

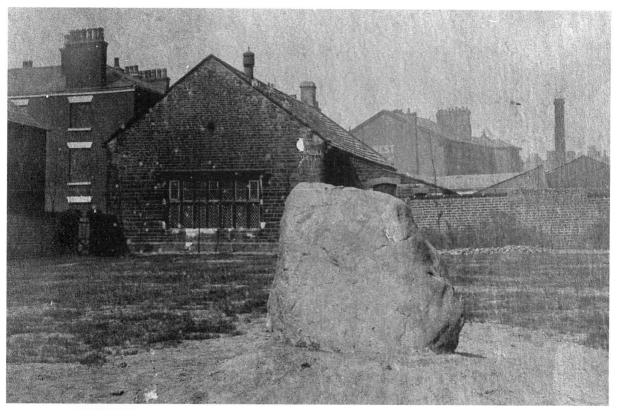

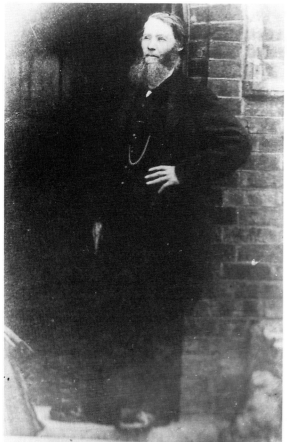

76 Brought from the Lake District by Ice-Age glaciers, this huge boulder lay for centuries in Crab Fields, just beyond Crab Lane (now Street). This became Quaker-owned land and in 1892, when streets were filling that area, the stone was moved. It is seen here newly established in the former Quaker burial ground whose 100 graves were usually unmarked. Three simply-inscribed gravestones do remain in one corner of what is now a pleasant small park entered from Shaw Street, and with the boulder at its centre. Catching the light, this appears as a white spot, well to the right of centre in the previous illustration.

77 Having begun his career as an Oxfordshire shepherd, Thomas Beecham's growing herbal skills led him to Wigan as a grocer/druggist and then, in 1859, to St Helens [53]. He prospered, moving to Westfield Street, outgrew adjoining workshop premises and built a small factory where his son Joseph joined him. Massive advertising in the 1880s paid off and a new building was commissioned for the expanding firm.

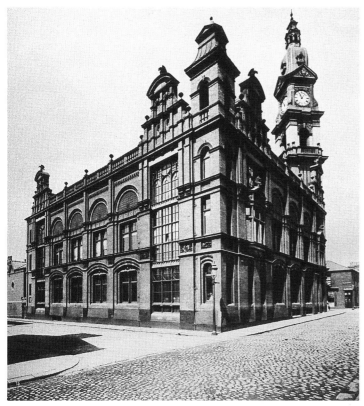

78 The architect Hugh Krowlaw designed this lavishly impressive building for Thomas and Joseph Beecham, seen here from Water Street shortly after its opening in 1887. Each side is different but in itself largely symmetrical—that fronting Silver Street has long been lost to view as, obliterating Silver Street itself, the works have been extended along Water Street. Lost, too, are the eagles, perched on the ornamental gables which cleverly obscured the chimney stacks behind them. Angled, at the corner with Westfield Street, the baroque clock tower adds an imaginative finish to the building, and a landmark to the town.

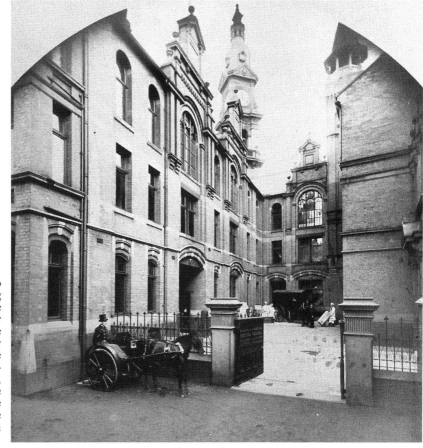

79 Silver Street ran parallel to Westfield Street—later being absorbed by the extension of the factory. From either one could enter the central courtyard, which the architect has treated with dignity and elegance. Here, in 1887, white clad employees are loading a horse-drawn van in the background, whilst, outside the railings, the groom is probably awaiting the Beecham children who were frequently driven to the works in just such a conveyance.

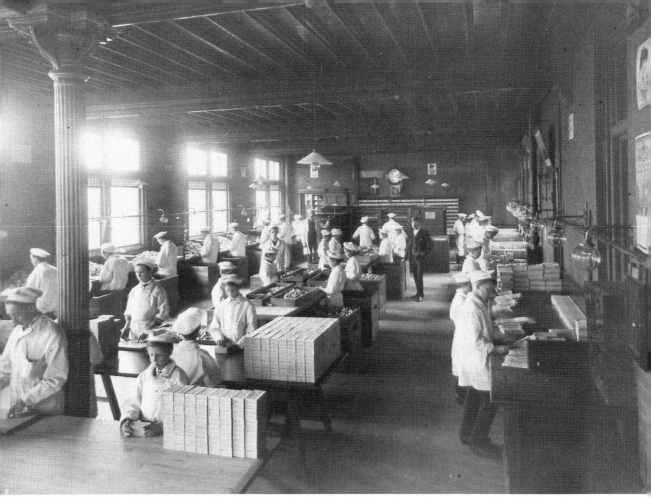

80 One could leave school at 10 in 1887, and some of Beecham's young white-hatted and coated pill packers seem little older than that. Kept busy shaping the boxes, then filling them with pills, they were allowed free tea and cocoa and, after hours, a billiards room. Internally, as this view of the pill-packing room shows, the factory was solidly structured and working conditions were good. It was lit by electricity, generated on the premises until town supplies reached Westfield Street in 1896. Joseph Beecham, knowledgeable chairman of the Electricity Committee 1900-17, delighted in the low production costs of the municipal power station.

81 This shows Beecham's warehouses in Lowe Street in 1925. Courtman's menswear shop now occupies the corner where the three men are standing. High on the upper floor the window glass still advertises 'Beecham's Pills'. Gone by 1925 is horse-drawn delivery.

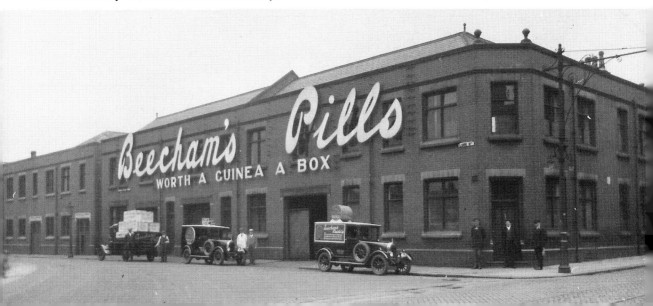

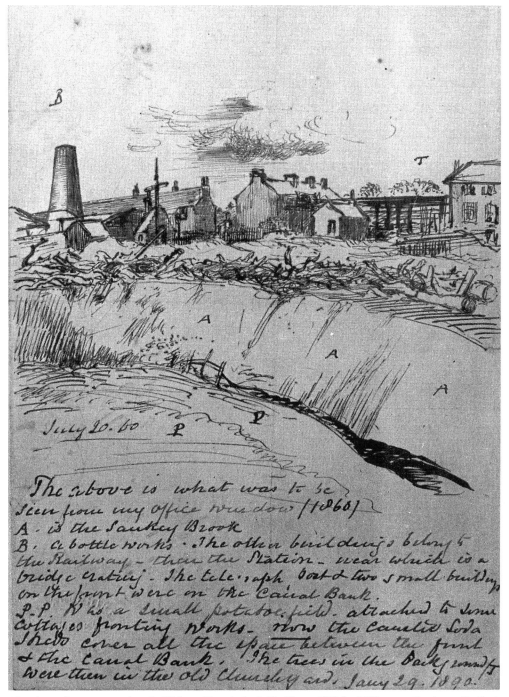

The sketch bears the handwritten annotations:

B

July 20. 60

The above is what was to be
seen from my office window [1860]
A. is the Sankey Brook
B. a bottle works. The other buildings belong to
the Railway — then the Station — near which is a
bridge grating. The telegraph post & two small buildings
on the front were on the Canal Bank.
P.P. Was a small potatoe field. attached to some
cottages fronting works — now the Caustic Soda
Sheds cover all the space between the front
& the Canal Bank. The trees in the back ground
were then in the old Churchyard. Jany 29. 1890.

82   As well as promoting St Helens Hospital, A.G. Kurtz [26] in 1878 gave the town its first public baths, built for his workforce in 1861 with a co-operative store next door.

The previous July (1860) he had sketched the view from his office window, adding the explanatory notes 30 years later. By then Salisbury Street's railway buildings had no trains and there was no potato patch.

Kurtz noted: 'The above is what was to be seen from my office window (1860). A. is the Sankey Brook, B. a bottle works. The other buildings belong to the Railway—then the Station— near which is a bridge grating. The telegraph post & two small buildings on the front were on the Canal Bank. P.P. Was a small potatoes field attached to some cottages fronting works. Now the Caustic Soda Sheds cover all the space between the front and the Canal Bank. The trees in the background were then in the old Churchyard. Jany 29, 1890.'

Kurtz died the following September.

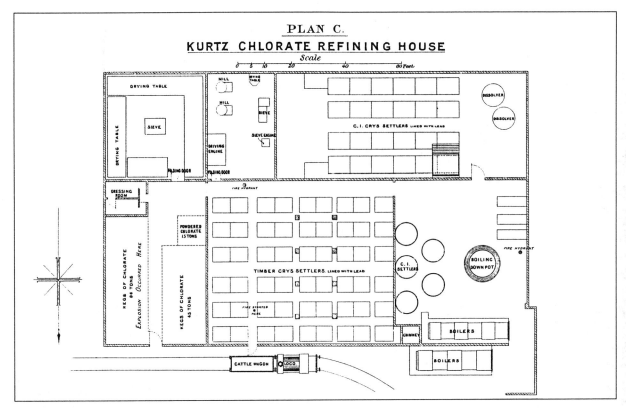

PLAN C.
KURTZ CHLORATE REFINING HOUSE

Scale

83, 84 & 85 The furthermost buildings of the Kurtz plant seen in [27] were beyond Warrington New Road, and built above a heap of chemical waste 40ft. high. They included the refining house in which the chlorate of potash—made on the canal-side site—crystallised in lead-lined wooden settling tanks. Once dried it was packed, as crystal or powder, into 5 cwt. kegs for despatch by rail. Empty kegs were returned, checked, and re-used.

On 12 May 1899 the third keg to be unloaded from a batch returned by Bryant and May slipped, rolling on to the second. A spark came as their nail-secured wooden hoops met. It ignited the chlorate-saturated wood of a settling tank.

Water was short—newly renewed works mains were being tested that day—and the fire spread to the roof timbers and thus to the topmost of the filled kegs in the adjacent store.

Minutes later the explosion came, felt 15 miles away, heard in Northwich and Oldham. Also built on waste heaps, the vitriol tanks of the adjoining Hardshaw Brook Chemical Works tore apart, their contents flowing into Warrington New Road. Across that road the gas holder, nearly three-quarters full, ruptured, fuelling a flame almost 700ft. high.

Amazingly, though the works was devastated, there were only five fatalities and ten people seriously injured. The end paper shows the area in which structural damage radiated from the refining house, whose layout is shown in 'Plan C'.

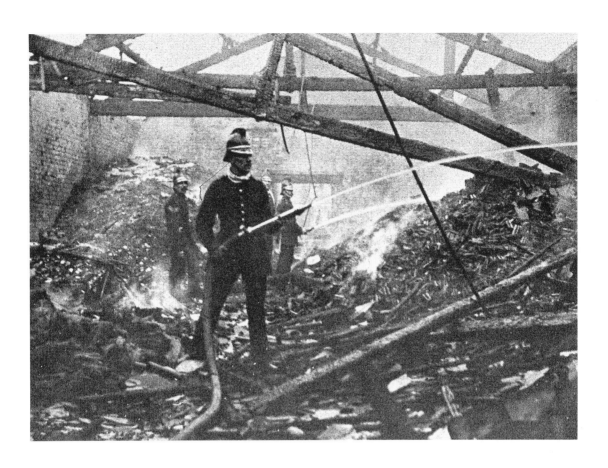

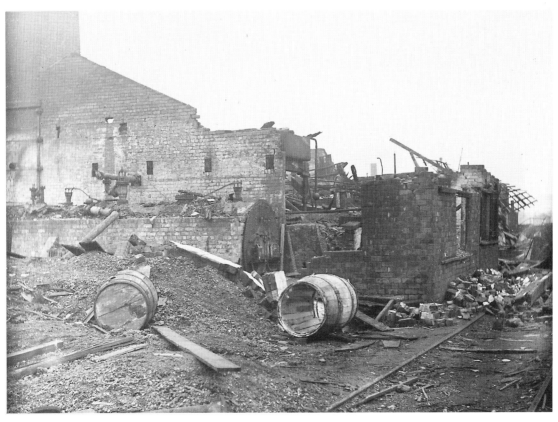

Before the N.H.S.

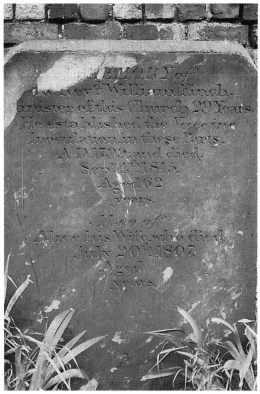

86 Buried at St Helens chapel of ease was the Rev. William Finch, minister there 1786-1815. Like many clergy of his time, he was concerned with scientific ideas. An insertion in the baptismal register for 1799 reads: 'David, son of David Scarborough, Clogger, St Helens. This child on the 17th November following was the first in these parts that was inoculated with vaccine matter. Per me W.Finch Minister'.

Mothers brought children to him to be vaccinated at the sessions he held at the workhouse on Moorflat. His headstone was photographed shortly before the Parish Church graveyard was cleared for the St Mary's Market development.

87 The original premises in Peasley Cross where St Helens Hospital opened in 1873 are still visible at the extreme right of this architect's drawing of the proposed extensions to the hospital, actually undertaken 1902-4. Labelled 'present administration' in the key, their future was seen as 'servants' quarters only'. The 'present ward' block was to have a twin, and a more handsome nurses' home than was actually built was to grace the front of the hospital, whilst a 'future' third ward was envisaged, and the extension was to include an operating theatre and a laundry. This would have delighted Mrs. Walker, the first matron, much criticised for her 'extravagant' insistence on clean linen. She would have marvelled that 449 cases were admitted in 1903 and 1,229 in 1913. There had been 37 in 1873.

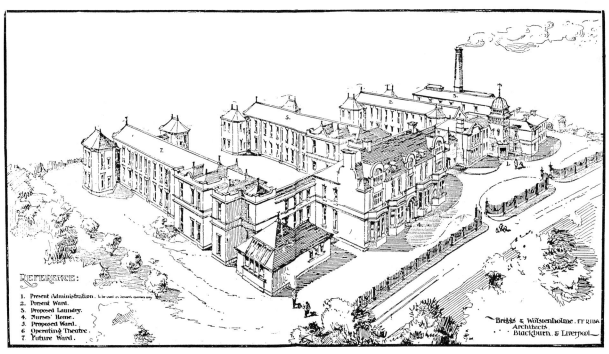

REFERENCE:
1. Present Administration. to be used as Servants quarters only
2. Present Ward.
3. Proposed Laundry.
4. Nurses' Home.
5. Proposed Ward.
6. Operating Theatre.
7. Future Ward.

Briggs & Wolstenholme. FF RIBA
Architects
Blackburn. & Liverpool

88 In January 1882, responding to a Holy Cross priest's plea, the foundress of the Poor Servants of the Mother of God Incarnate, Fanny Margaret Taylor (Mother Magdalen), came with four nuns to serve St Helens' poor. Living upstairs in this George Street house, at the corner of Raven Passage (where its former door is now positioned), they used the lower rooms for women too ill to be tended at home, and rented a nearby house to care for men and boys. Larger premises were soon needed.

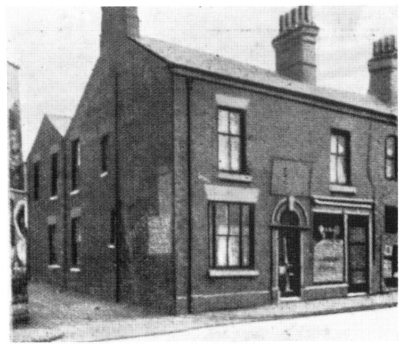

89 Re-built in 1840, after the Cotham family had moved to Springfield, Eccleston (later a Carmelite convent), Hardshaw Hall was leased to the sisters. It was opened by Cardinal Manning on 15 September 1884, as the Providence Free Hospital. It soon proved too small. Funded by Peter Middlehurst, the 1888 wing on the right was built. Its nearer section with a lanterned first-floor operating theatre was added later. Despite many extensions (including the nurses' home—now Providence Court), the former hall remained the heart of the 'Prov', whose closure in 1982 caused much local regret. The hall survives as the Grosvenor Housing Association's head office.

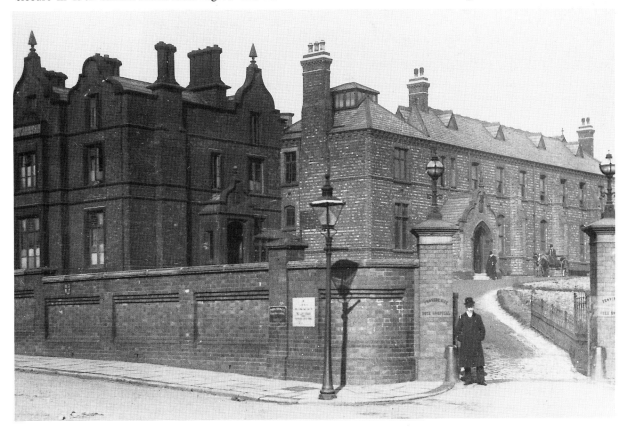

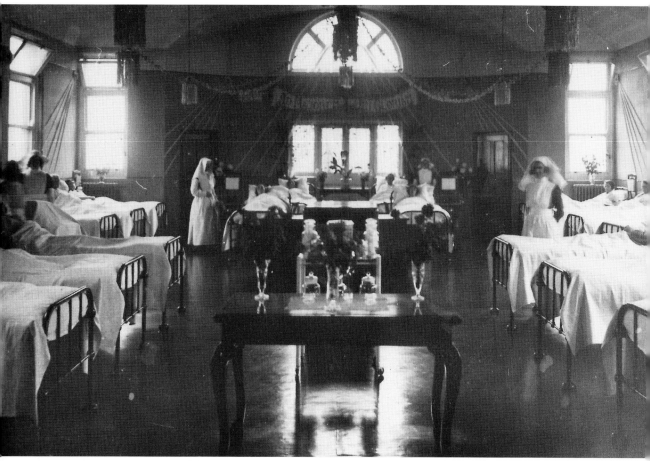

90 Seen decorated for the hospital's Golden Jubilee in 1932, this women's ward exudes cleanliness, with its gleaming floor, immaculate albeit tight-packed beds and the nurses' snowy well-starched linen.

Church and Chapel

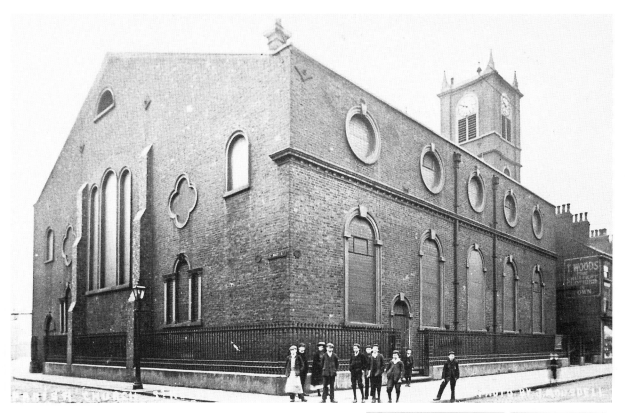

91 The 18th-century successor to St Elyn's Chapel was extended sideways in 1816, covering the old burying ground. Land to its south-east, bought from Bamber Gascoigne, one of the chapel trustees, was consecrated for burial. The resultant bulky, square-shaped church, thereafter dedicated to St Mary, contrasted oddly with its slender tower.

In this early 20th-century photograph can be seen the clock given by James Radley, mayor 1873-6, and the east window, restored after the Kurtz explosion.

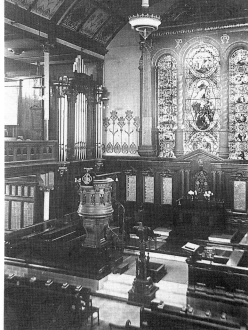

92 Among the improvements made to pews, galleries and flooring in the Parish Church in 1888 was the creation of a new chancel, its floor three inches above the general level, with new choir stalls, and the pulpit presented by Mr. and Mrs. Tinker [27]. By 1901 when the eagle lectern was given in Queen Victoria's memory, electric lighting had been installed, the organ improved and the east window restored.

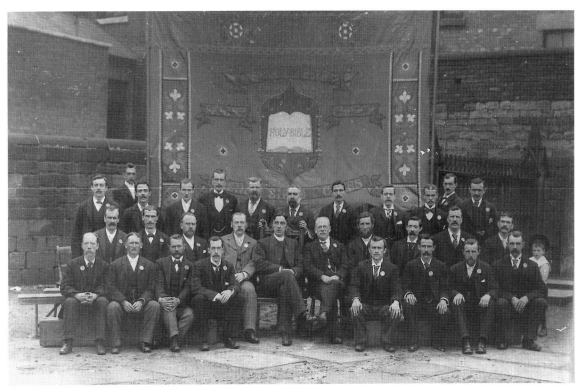

93 Founded in 1888, the Parish Church Men's Bible Class met every Sunday for over a century. Its second leader (1891-1904), the Rev. J.W. Willink, is seen here with a handful of its many members. Usually about 450 would come, but his largest class numbered 2,395 when the Mayor, Council and Volunteer battalions attended to mark Victoria's Diamond Jubilee. To mark its own jubilees, the Class presented the church with a handsome carved oak reredos and a magnificent organ case, both designed by Caroe.

94 Probably an electrical fault caused fire to break out in the Parish Church roof early on 2 December 1916. Both the town's and Pilkington's fire brigades fought the blaze, two firemen being lucky that the bell, falling from the tower, merely knocked their hose from them. By dawn little survived. In May 1917 as men dismantled the ruins the 18th-century nave's roof-line showed clearly on the tower, and the circular windows of the later north wall had been bricked up.

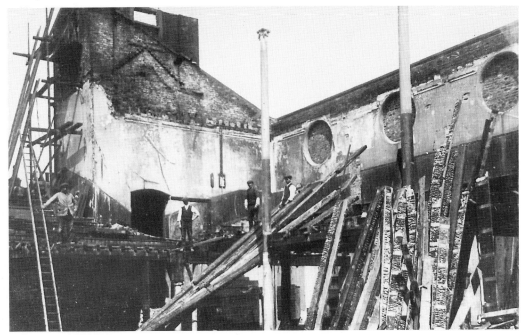

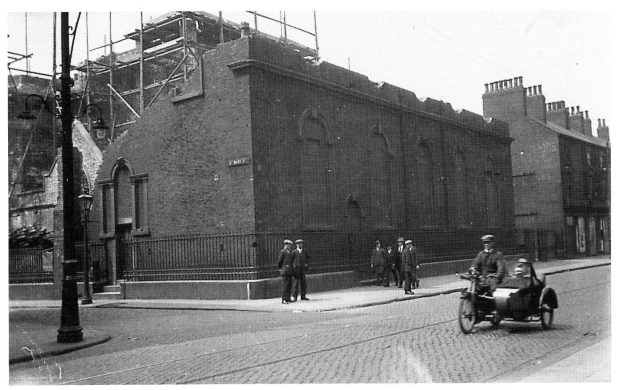

95 Seen from the far side of Church Street, looking towards the corner of St Mary's Street, St Helens' new parish church is taking shape within the protective wall of the old. It is set further back from Church Street, as the scaffolding round the tower, at its north-east corner, shows. The work of W.D. Caroe and dedicated to St Helen, the impressive church was consecrated on 7 November 1926, so ending the congregation's decade of worship at the Town Hall.

96 This view of St Thomas's Church in Westfield Street, dated 1909 by an unknown hand, feels both strange and familiar. Was the tower of Peter Greenall's 1839 church still standing then? Much has been altered. The 1890-1 chancel by Aldridge and Deacon remains today but little else has survived the 1910 rebuilding work and the 1960 fire.

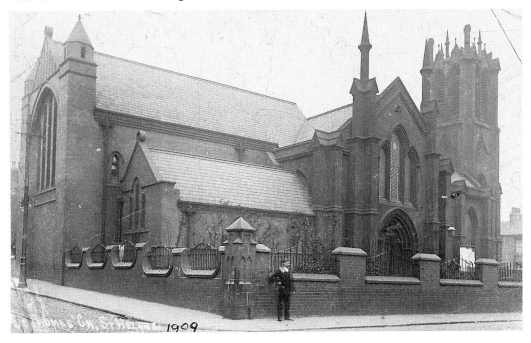

97 Links with North Wales and Anglesey, begun when the Parys Mine Company started smelting copper at Ravenhead in the 1780s, were maintained as men, often accompanied by their families, came to seek jobs in the various copper works and coal pits. Some met to worship in Welsh. Appropriately, since its side walls are made of blocks of copper slag (a useful by-product of smelting and refining found in many Sutton walls, and two local churches), a Welsh-speaking congregation has worshipped at this former Methodist chapel in Sutton Oak since 1893.

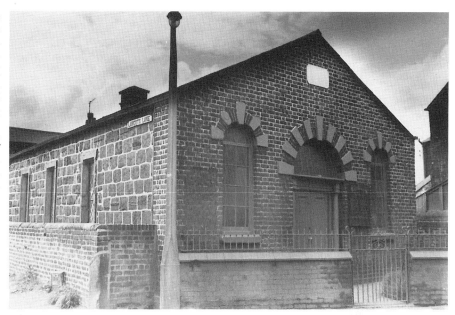

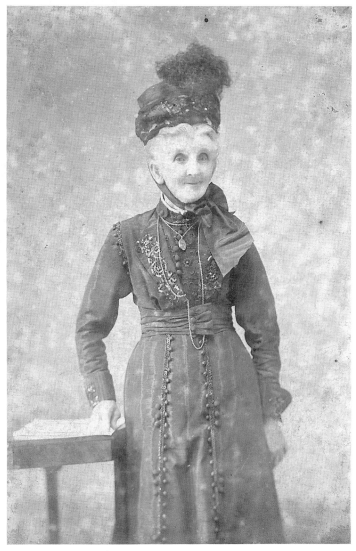

98 Youngsters learnt Welsh at Sunday School and, since the undenominational chapel has had no resident minister, would have been baptised when visiting Welsh-speaking clergy came for anniversary or funeral services. When Mrs. Mary Davies of Sutton Road, a member for 45 years, died in 1926 aged 78, the chapel was full for her funeral. Much respected, a miner's wife with miner sons, all of them important chapel members, she is seen here in her chapel-going attire.

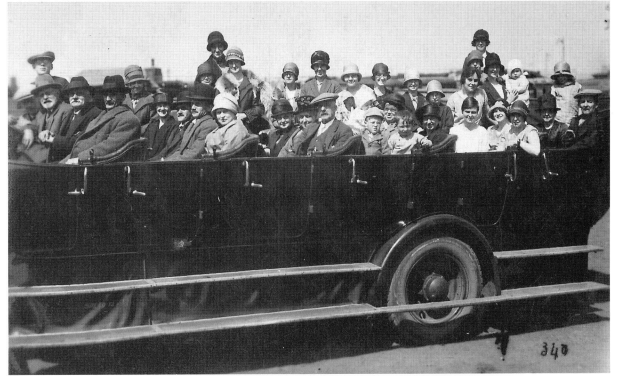

99 & 100 Outings and choral events were highlights of the chapel year. All available chapel members seem to have supported this Sunday School outing, for which, as for many other local groups' excursions, charabancs were provided by James Bridge & Sons of Ashcroft Street.

Both these vehicles have reached Southport. One, with the adults, has a removable folding hood, and a separate access door for each row of passengers. The other seems more childproof and stands in front of the former Winter Gardens (now a Safeway store). Where, though, are the buckets and spades?

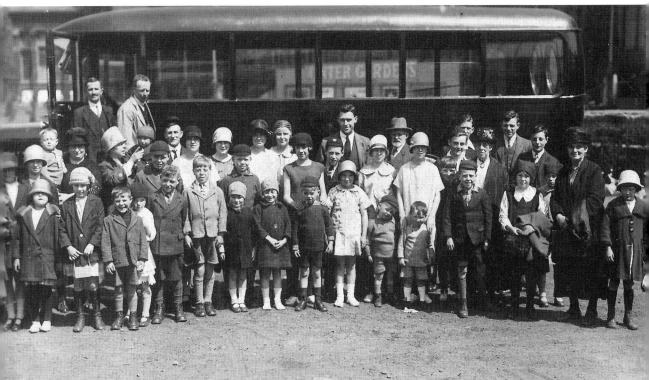

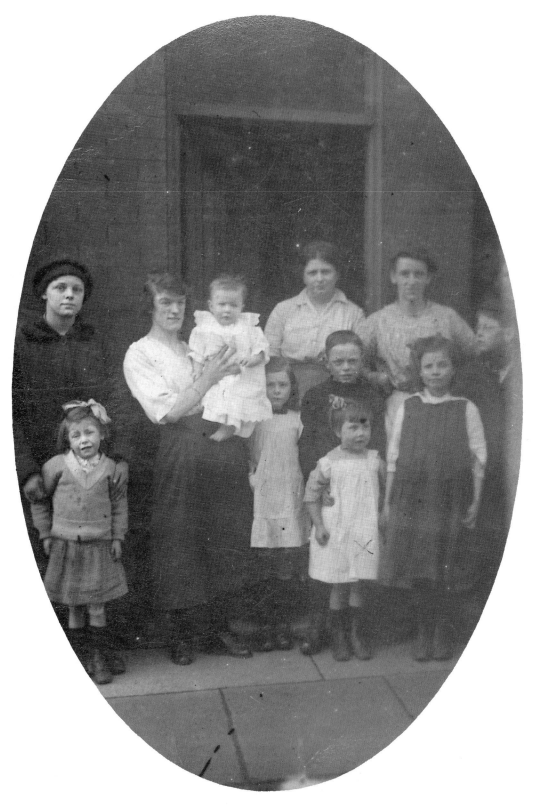

101 A small Sunday scholar (marked X) holds her sister's hand at the front of this group of Sutton neighbours, photographed during the coal strike of 1921. Despite the starched and snowy frills the baby is a boy, who like his fellows would not be 'breeched' before he was at least a sturdy toddler.

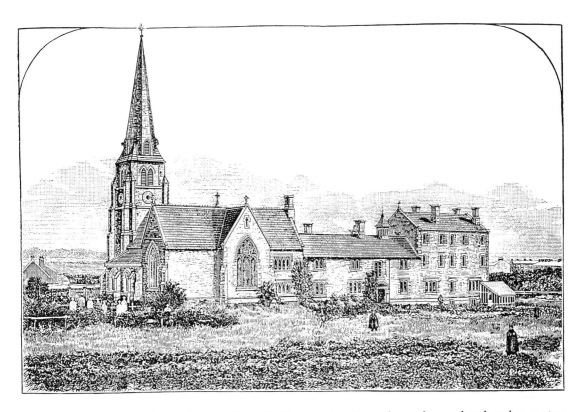

102 & 103 Entitled 'St. Anne's Retreat, Sutton', this engraving shows the sandstone church and monastery constructed by John Middlehurst on land between Gerards Lane and the St Helens Railway (see map below). Both site and building stone were given to the Passionists by self-made John Smith, engineer to the Railway. He also gave his home, Mount Pleasant, which bordered the curved track linking the St Helens and Liverpool-Manchester lines, to become a convent. Smith died, in 1862, at St Anne's Villa, near the church and monastery completed a decade earlier. Sadly, mining subsidence caused the demolition of the tower and, more recently, the rest of the church, whose modern successor was opened in 1973.

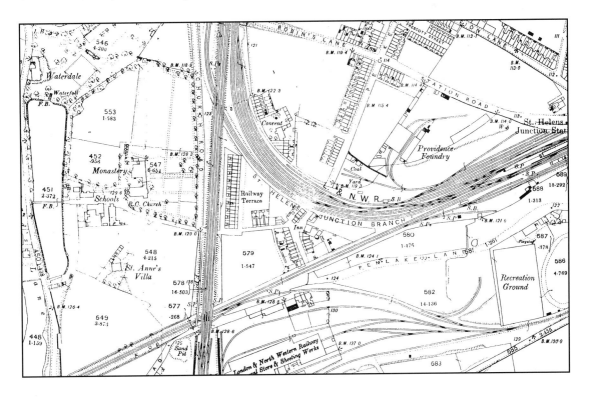

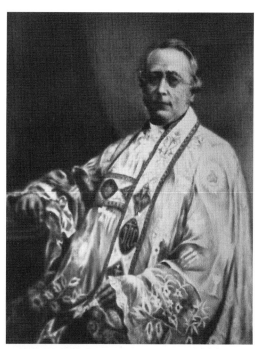

104 The new Town Hall was the venue, in August 1877, for the presentation of this lifesize portrait of himself to Father Thomas Ullathorne, S.J. The event marked the quarter centenary of his coming to Lowe House, and the esteem in which he was held. Arriving at Lowe House when famine-created hardship in Ireland and the availability of work in St Helens were drawing Irish Catholics to the town, Ullathorne's achievements in expanding church provision and erecting Catholic schools were inestimable. His elaborate surplice and stole were gifts from Mary, Marchioness Stapleton-Bretherton, the patroness of Holy Cross. The portrait's current whereabouts is uncertain.

105 Divided vertically by North Road and Baldwin Street, this photograph shows near its centre the Capitol cinema which opened in 1929 and, at the Duke Street/College Street corner, the former manse demolished in 1932. Further up North Road, St Mary's Lowe House, completed in 1930, stands out splendidly with its presbytery to its left and then its school. The vast playground also served the Volunteers, their Mill Street H.Q. being at its other end. Bottom centre is the Co-op roof. On Corporation Street, slanting from bottom right, are the Mining School, the white-stepped terrace of [54] and the Central Station, its goods yard to the rear.

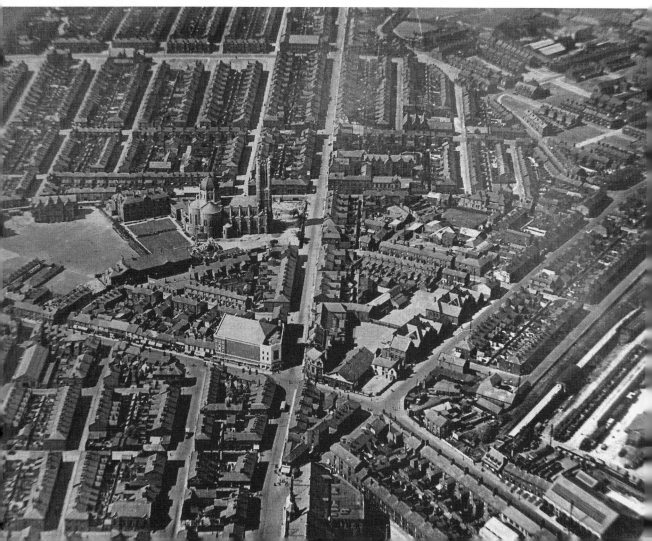

106 Holy Cross Church is said to have been built (1861-2) from stone quarried underground at Crank Caverns. Its architect was J.J. Scholes. This photograph just pre-dates the building of the People's Palace (1892-3) on the empty site in the foreground. It shows the Hall Street tramsheds of 1880 and track turning that way from Corporation Street. Faint in the background are the twin spires of Tolver Street Presbyterian Church of 1868 (now a furniture warehouse). A carriage works, shirt factory and theatre workshop are some of the rôles played by the building whose presence is revealed by its large dark shadow.

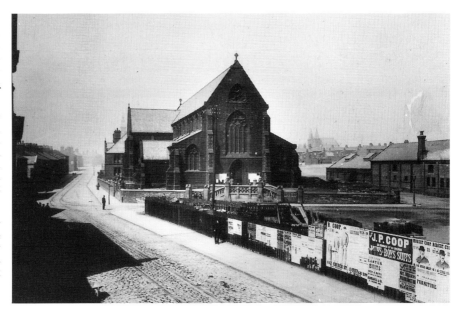

107 In October 1906 a week's celebrations marked the centenary of the Congregational Sunday School of which Dr. William Pilkington had been the first treasurer.

Earlier, on August Bank Holiday, the scholars joined by those from the daughter church at Newtown had walked in procession to festivities at Windle Hall Farm, Hard Lane.

Those seen here are at the bottom of Dentons Green Lane. In starched whiteness, with spectacular hats and gleaming shoes, the young ladies walk in pairs between the tramlines. The houses nearby have gone, but the shops glimpsed between the banners survive.

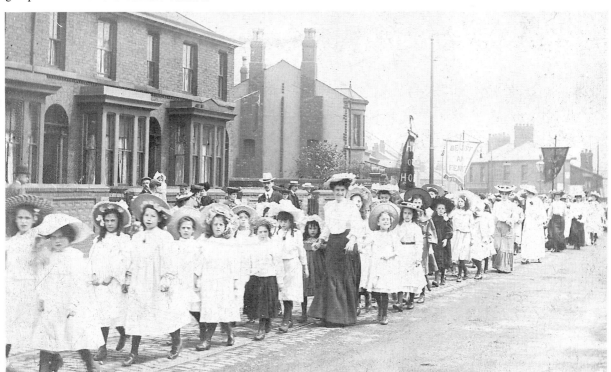

Schools and Scholars

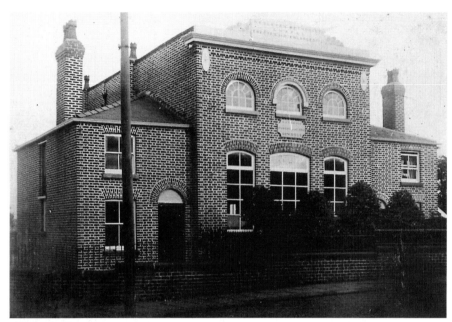

108 A filling station now stands where, in 1811, the Nuttalls [46] provided this combined school and chapel, plus cottages for the chapel keeper and the school mistress. Girls attended during the week, while boys, usually in employment, attended on Sundays.

Though enlarged in 1840, by the 1870s more space was needed, but mining subsidence was affecting the building. (Note the tie-rods.) As a result of the congregation's financial and physical efforts (which included blasting away rock), a new chapel was opened in 1883. The 1811 building lost its junior scholars to Govett Road in 1897, but remained as an infant school until the late 1960s.

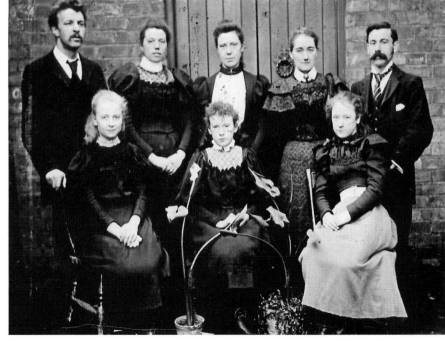

109 Appointed in 1897, not long after the Govett Road building was opened, Henry Charles Guy was head of Nutgrove Methodist School until his death in 1932. Photographed *c*.1900, he stands top left beside his colleagues. Barely older than their charges, three pupil teachers, who could begin their four-year apprenticeship at 13, are seated at the front. [See 126]

110 Son of the schoolmaster of the former Free Grammar School on Eccleston Hill, Richard John Seddon, an ex-apprentice from Daglish's foundry, emigrated in 1864, settling in New Zealand. He became involved in local government, was elected to parliament and, much respected, served as Prime Minister from 1893 until his death in 1906. His ministry enfranchised women and introduced old age pensions. While visiting England, and St Helens, for Edward VII's coronation, he received the freedom of the Borough. His portrait hangs in the Mayor's Robing Room, and he is commemorated by a plaque at his birthplace, and choir stalls at Christ Church, Eccleston.

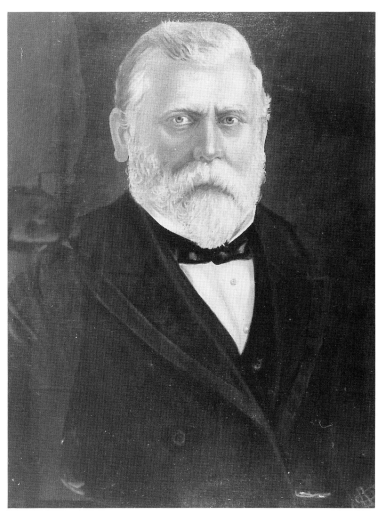

111 The foundation stone of the Wesleyan Day Schools was laid on 8 June 1854. Erected by George Harris on the former bowling green of the *Red Lion Hotel*, the building was L-shaped. The boys' school faced Waterloo Street, and the girls' and infants' with the adjoining schoolmaster's house fronted Milk Street [53].

Much later, from 1946, the Commerce Department of the Technical College—which had long outgrown its Gamble accommodation—occupied the Wesleyan schools. In the late '50s the college began to spread from Water Street, absorbing the Wesleyan site in the early '60s.

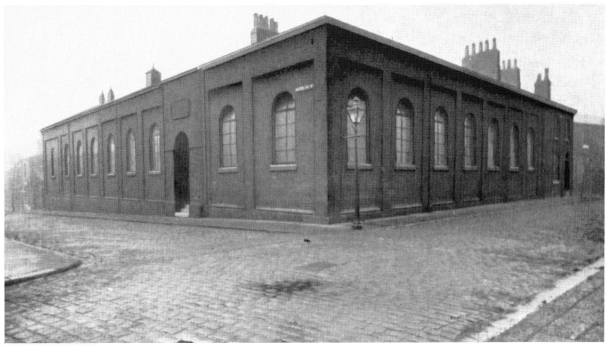

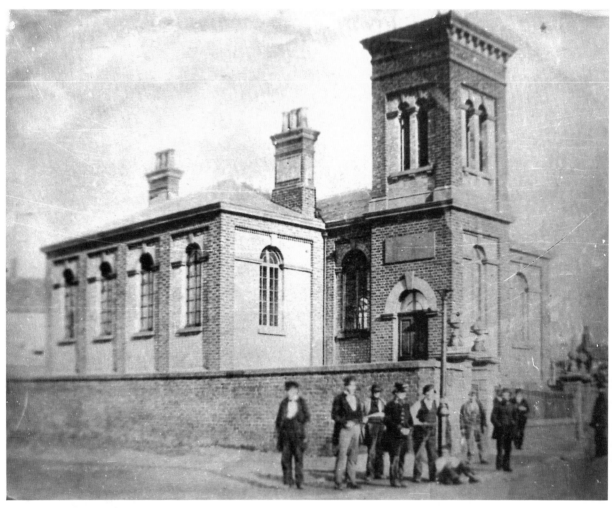

112 Still known as 'Lacey's' even when the Y.M.C.A. was built beside it in 1903, this boys' school in North Road stood on the site later occupied by the Central Modern School. It had been erected by the Cowley Trustees when the lease of land at Shaw Street to the railway in 1856 boosted their income. Newton Lacey (brother of the Libraries Committee Chairman, H.R. Lacey) was the Trust's headmaster from 1846 until the Trustees' 1875 scheme, requiring qualified teachers, caused his resignation. The photograph is undated. Were these young gentlemen Lacey's pupils?

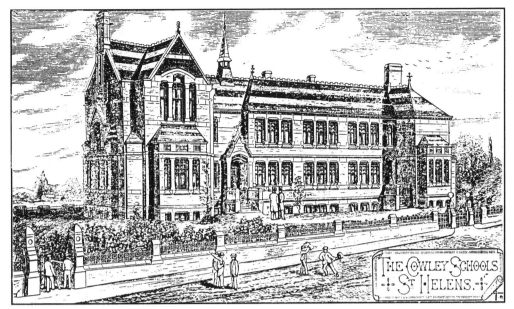

113 The Sarah Cowley Trustees employed Henry Sumner, architect of the 1876 Town Hall, when the Cowley Schools were built in Cowley Hill Lane. Opened in 1882, the building accommodated 150 boys (note the cricket bats and the top-hatted masters) and, at its right-hand end, 100 girls. Evening classes took place there until the Gamble Institute was opened.

In 1912 the girls had the building to themselves for the boys moved to the newly-built 'South Block' next door. This, too, the girls inherited when the boys moved to Hard Lane in 1930.

114 Like most Moss Bank buildings, that which served as mission church and school was stone built. Gilbert Greenall (Peter's brother) gave the land for it and its adjoining schoolmaster's house to 'the minister and churchwardens' of the 'new parish of St Helens' in 1855. One Saturday in 1865 John Ansdell, solicitor and school trustee, enabled 100 Liverpool naturalists to take tea at the school after botanising at Carr Mill. By 1895, the school-leaving age for these Moss Bank pupils, some of whose descendants are still Moss Bankers, had reached eleven.

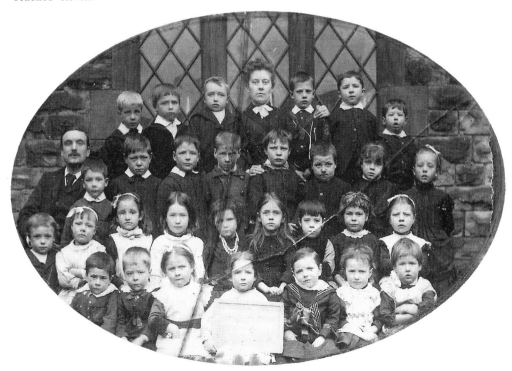

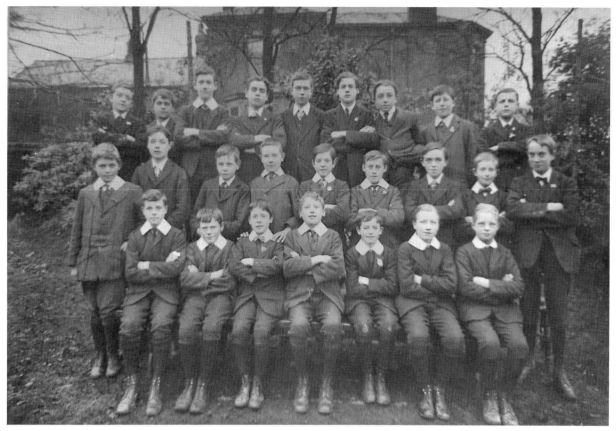

115 In 1915 when this class was photographed the Catholic Grammar School had 112 pupils. In the background is the St George's Road house where it had begun in 1899 (41 years after Notre Dame School opened at 10 Hardshaw Street). By 1915 West Park House, in whose grounds the group poses, had been bought, becoming the residence of the de la Salle community who had taken the school over in 1911. Having expanded here and over the site of neighbouring Eccleston Place, West Park School moved to Alder Hey Road in 1965. Now a mixed comprehensive, De la Salle High School occupies the former Notre Dame premises at Mill Brow.

116 The Elms in Cowley Hill Lane, once the home of Thomas Brewis, a former Town Clerk, housed Cowley Schools' Preparatory Department 1918-30, becoming increasingly over-crowded. This tight-packed group, Prep. D of 1928, includes a future doctor, solicitor, motor cycle champion and professor of economic history—Tom Merrick, Bert Fairclough, Geoff Duke and John Harris.

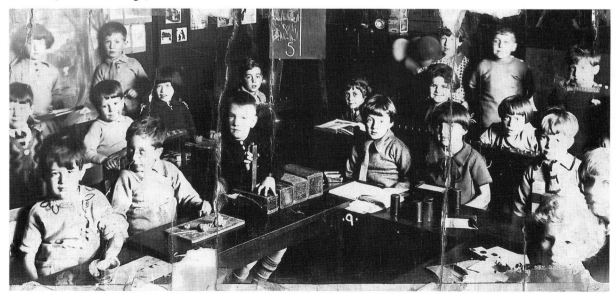

Around the Square

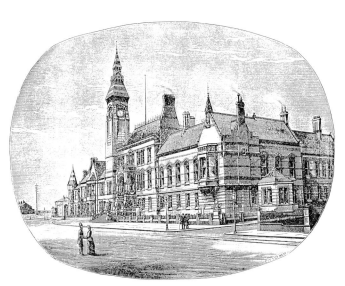

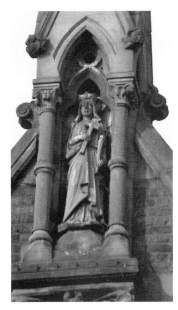

117 & 118 In June 1876, facing what was then Cotham Street, St Helens' new Town Hall, designed by Henry Sumner of Liverpool, was officially opened. The lavish porch, surmounted by the borough coat of arms, led to the principal floor with its large assembly room and, to the far right, the bay-windowed Mayor's Parlour, above which a statue of St Helen stood, high in the gable. To the left, with its own entrance was the magistrates' court room, linked to the police offices and cells below. The entirely panelled Council Chamber, placed centrally two floors up, overlooked the porch.

119 As industrial growth brought an influx of strangers to the townships, traditional law and order resources—constable, stocks, dilapidated lock-up—grew increasingly inadequate. Troops were needed when miners struck in 1831. Improvements came. The 1839 Town Hall provided a bridewell and a house for the constable. That autumn the Lancashire county force was set up and in 1840 a detachment was based in St Helens, with Hardshaw's former constable as its superintendent. Local policing, long wanted, was only achieved in 1887. The 20 members of the borough force seen here joined at its inception. All had served for 25 years when this photograph was taken in 1912. Last to retire, in January 1919, was Alan Bradley (back row, 2nd right).

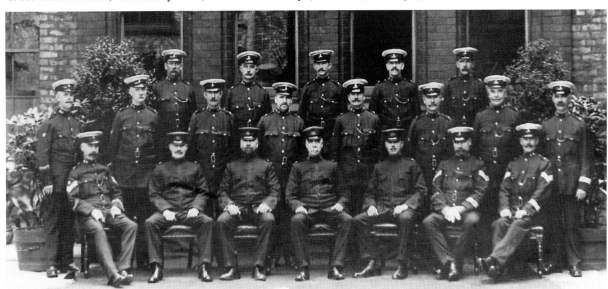

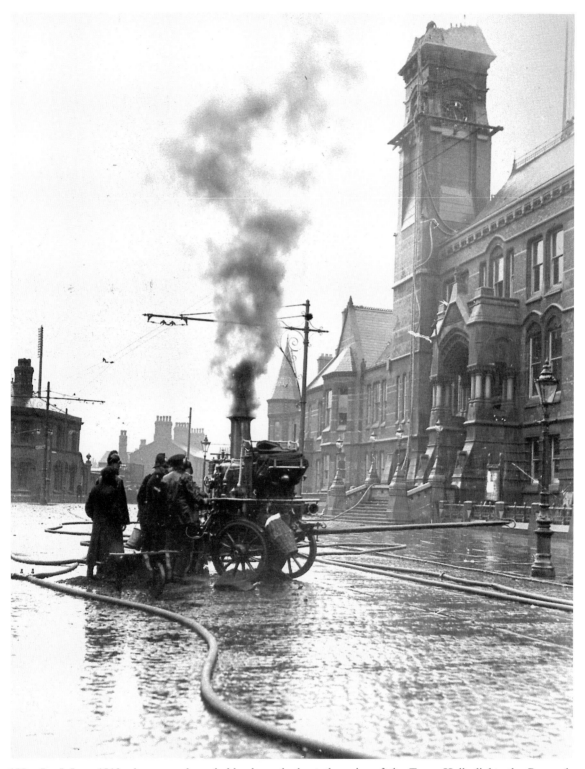

120 On 9 June 1913 when a workman's blowlamp had set the spire of the Town Hall alight, the Borough and Pilkington's fire brigades tackled the blaze together. Pilkington's fire escape was placed against the tower; hoses were connected and taken to the top, and, below, were attached to the town's new motor fire engine. It failed to work, and this 'large' horse-drawn steam engine was brought from the Sheet Works. Here it is seen in the aftermath of the fire, still emitting smoke and steam. The hose snakes up the tower to the point where the spire has fractured and a solitary fireman works on.

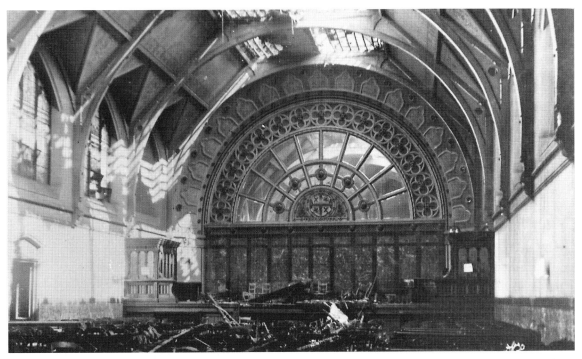

121 After the fire, sunlight slants through the broken roof and charred timbers lie on the floor of the Town Hall Assembly Room. Here, in his father Joseph's mayoralty, young Thomas Beecham had made his debut, conducting the Hallé orchestra; here David Gamble and Richard Seddon had received the freedom of the Borough; here guests had lunched in splendour when the Central Railway was opened; here, in 1905, so many came to hear Madame Clara Butt sing that some had even been accommodated on the platform.

122 To modern eyes Pilkington's 1910 works fire brigade seems somewhat inadequate. The immaculate horses and their drivers were more accustomed to conveying the directors in their carriages. By 1912 the brigade had its own fire station (replaced in 1936) at the corner of Canal Street and Bridgewater Street. In both the Town Hall and the Parish Church fires its members greatly assisted the town brigade. This, based at the Town Hall, was from 1893-1938 under police management—some constables doubling as firemen.

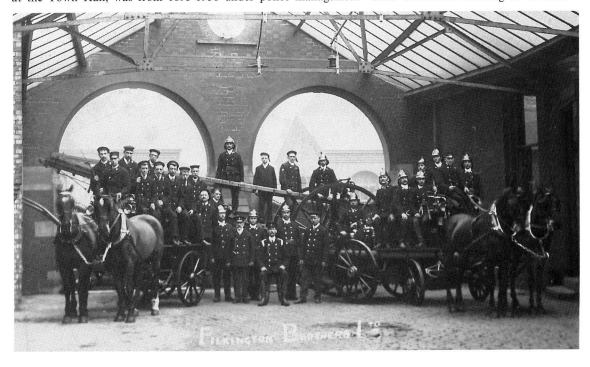

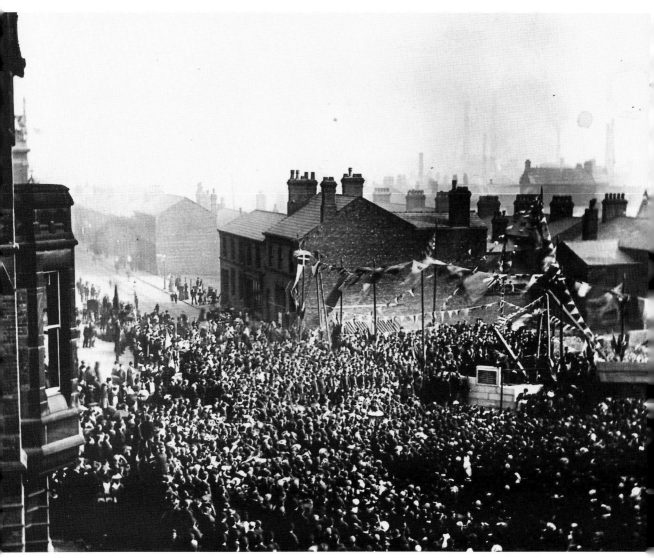

123   In April 1893 the Corporation gladly accepted David Gamble's offered plot of land at the corner of Hardshaw Street and Corporation Street and £20,000 to erect a free public library and technical school thereon. Here, on 2 October 1894, David Gamble stands beside the foundation stone he is laying, with the dignitaries on a temporary platform behind him. The sun shines on the crowd gathered for this major local event—but it and the breeze briskly blowing the flags seem unable to dispel the industrial murk obscuring all but the nearest houses in the background.

124   (*top right*) The architects Briggs and Wolstenholme, of Liverpool and Blackburn, provided Reference, Lending and Reading room facilities for the library. In this picture it seems largely the Libraries Committee who are caught by the camera. Their octogenarian chairman, H.R. Lacey, sits at the right (not yet the J.P. he is to become at 90), with David Gamble's hand on his shoulder. Above the librarian's head is a framed drawing of the building. The panelling of her desk nowadays lines the Local History and Archives Library upstairs.

125   (*bottom right*) From 1854 until 1925 browsing was an unknown pleasure for St Helens library users, access to books being restricted to the staff only.

Here, sunlight slants across the original library interior from the low central roof of the Gamble Institute—a quality building with its tiled pillars and corridor, parquet floor and impressive door casings. To the right, reminiscent of an old-fashioned railway booking office, are the windows through which books were issued.

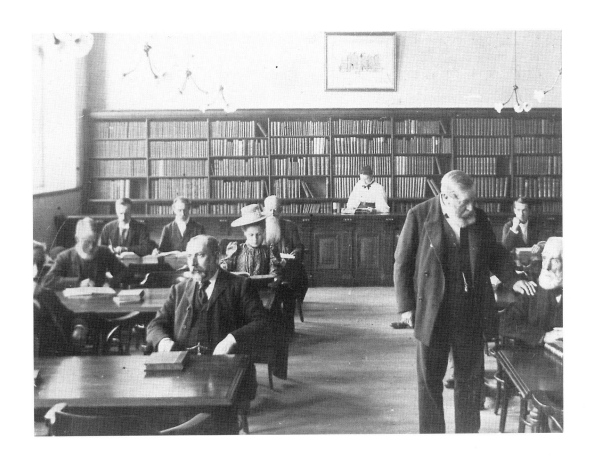

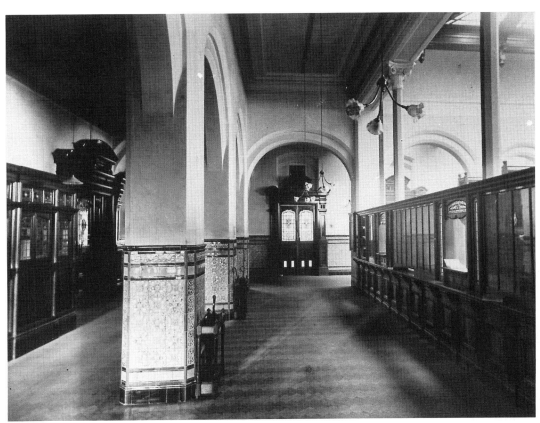

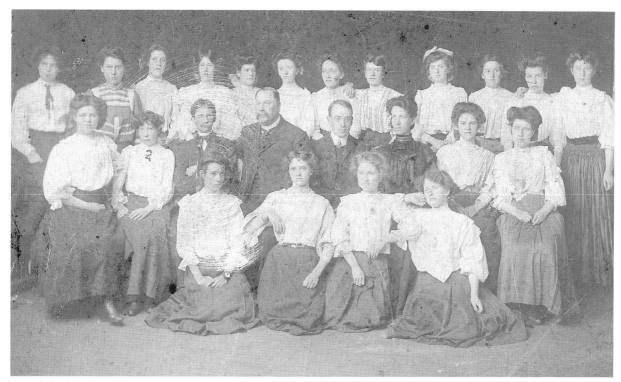

126 Until 1898 St Helens' pupil teachers were instructed outside school hours, usually by their head-teachers. That April a Pupil Teachers' Centre was established at the Gamble Institute. Initially, its two teachers had 115 students attending at least four half-days a week, and split into four year-groups. This senior group were photographed with their teachers in the early 1900s.

127 By January 1902 days were numbered for the houses that, when it was built, stood opposite the 'Gamble', as the new institute quickly became known, whose gables are just visible. To the right the offices later known as the Prudential Buildings (also by Briggs and Wolstenholme) are under construction.

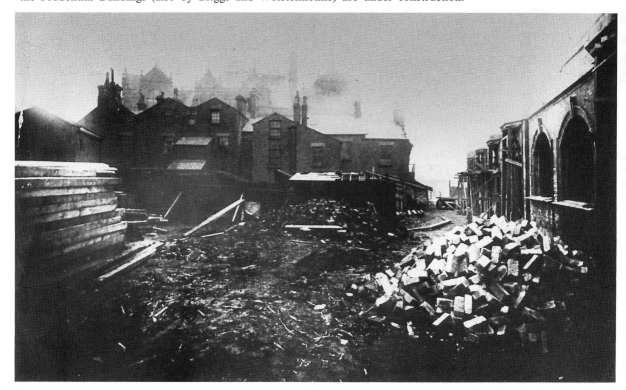

Getting About

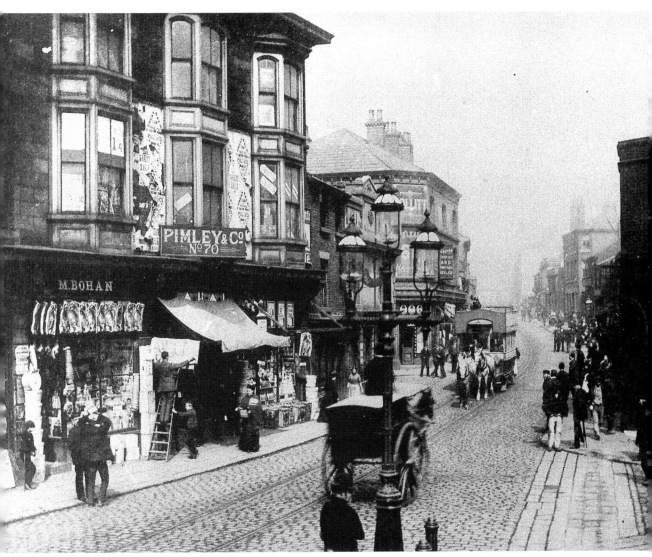

128 St Helens' first horse-drawn trams began to operate from Ormskirk Street to Prescot in 1879. Croppers Hill presented a problem, and spare horses were stabled at the *Feathers* at the corner of Eccleston Street. The hourly service was doubled on Monday and Saturday afternoons (Market days), when the hourly service to Toll Bar terminated at Prescot instead.

This Prescot-bound tram is approaching the bottom of Bridge Street. It has passed Pollitt's, the hatters, on the corner of Water Street and is beside the *A1 Vaults*. The clogger's, next door, is dwarfed by the larger premises of two grocers, their wares displayed outside, one each side of the clothiers, Pimley and Co.

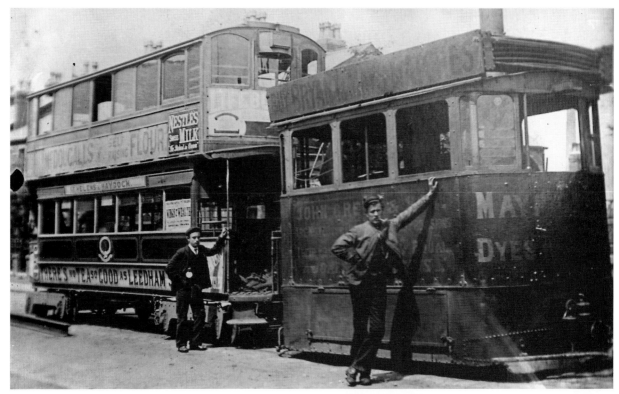

129 Nine steam tram engines served St Helens between 1893 and 1900. The direction board shows this engine and its trailer (in which the passengers travelled) were operating on the St Helens-Haydock route.

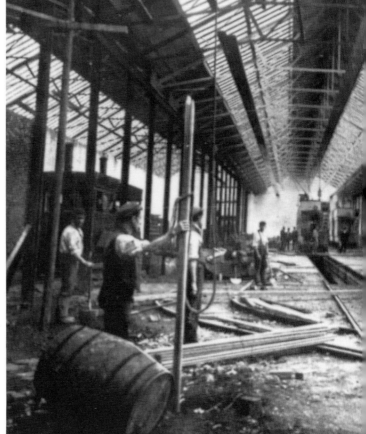

130 In 1898 the Hall Street Tram Depot was adapted and much widened to accommodate the new fleet of 36 electric tramcars. The depot had been built in 1880 to house the horse trams of the St Helens and District Tramways on land purchased from the Walmesley-Cotham family. In this photograph, alterations are in hand. The engine for a steam tram can be seen on the left. In the background is one of the new trams; these began to run to Toll Bar in August 1898.

Modern visitors will find the depot is now the home of the North West Transport Museum. It had served the town's transport until February 1986.

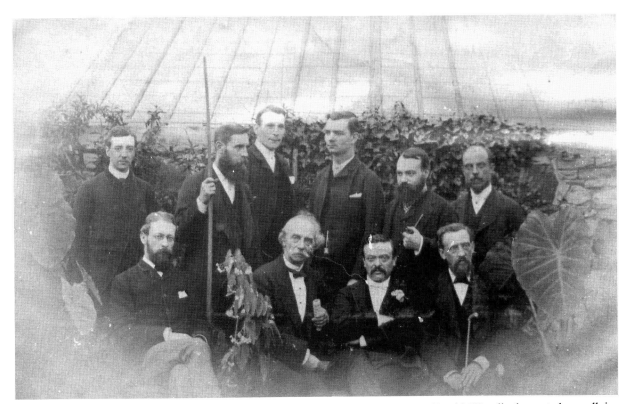

131 Mr. David Woodlock, seated, scroll in hand, ran the art class of the town's Association for the Pursuit of Science, Literature and Art. This met 1883-5 in a Salisbury Street house provided by its president Mr. R.G. Brook (who sits at his left) and later in Wolverhampton House, Mr. Brook's hardware business premises and one-time home. The Society members seen here include (holding a long cue) James Brockbank, an Ormskirk Street shoemaker, whose historical notes and listing of local events remain invaluable.

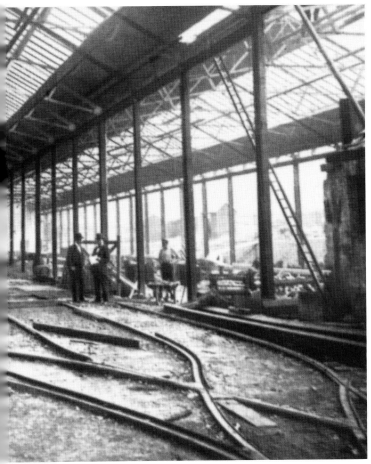

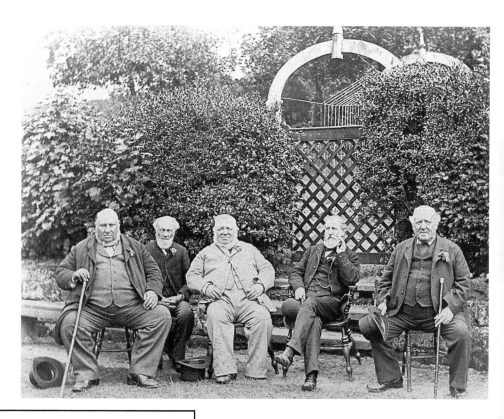

132 & 133 R.G. Brook liked photography and took this picture (*above*) on a Lymm visit. His home, Wolverhampton House, had been built by 31-stone John Whittaker, seated at the left, whose other works included Sutton Oak Plate Glass Works (later Sidac), Boundary Road Baths and many chimneys. Wheelwright and blacksmith 22-stone Joseph Jackson, after whom Jackson Street was named, made chains and ironwork for local collieries and sits at the centre. Glass flattener, 18-stone Charles Rigby, builder J. Roughsedge and a Mr. W. Gardiner complete the party.

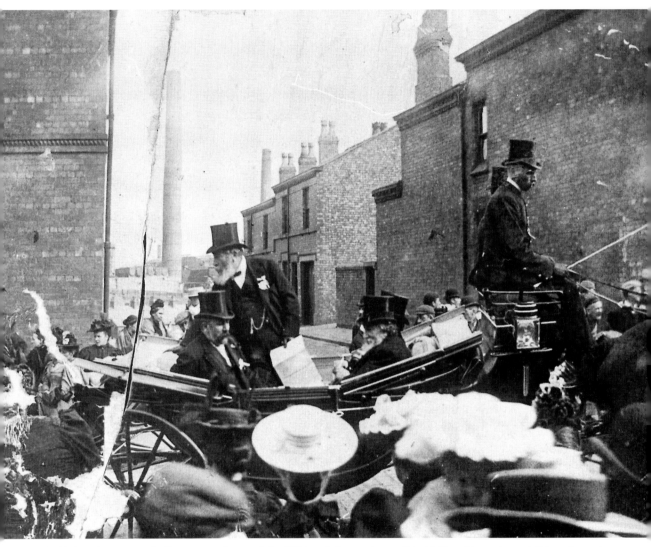

134 St Helens became a Parliamentary borough in 1884 and the next year David Gamble, a staunch Liberal, made his only bid for election to the Commons. This undated photograph of him canvassing was probably taken then. If so, seated by him is Francis Dixon-Nuttall. Gamble lost by 57 votes, the town's Irish having followed Parnell's instruction to vote Conservative, and Henry Seton-Karr became St Helens' first M.P.

In Town and Country

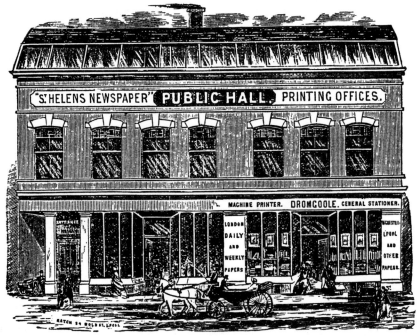

B. A. DROMGOOLE,
GENERAL
Printer, Bookseller, & Wholesale Stationer

Public Hall, Hardshaw-st., & 17 & 19, Liverpool-road,
ST. HELENS,
ALSO AT WATERLOO-STREET, WIDNES.

Machine, Letterpress, Copperplate, and Lithographic Printing,
ENGRAVING, BOOKBINDING, &c.

Proprietor of the St. Helens Newspaper & Advertiser
Published every Tuesday and Saturday.—Established 1860.

Bibles, Church Services, Missals, Prayer Books, &c. Schools supplied with every
description of Books, Slates, Pencils, &c.

135 Apart from the lettering, the upper frontage of what is now the Halifax
Building Society is unaltered. Separately housed, the press was reached via the
passage to the left. The high gallery once surrounding it may be recalled as part
of Hart's store. Bernard Augustus Dromgoole campaigned through editorials and
meetings in the 'Public Hall' (entered by the door on the left) against local electoral
abuses and laggardly officialdom and, equally fervently, for the town's borough
status, museum, parks and footpaths, and to build Sacred Heart Church.

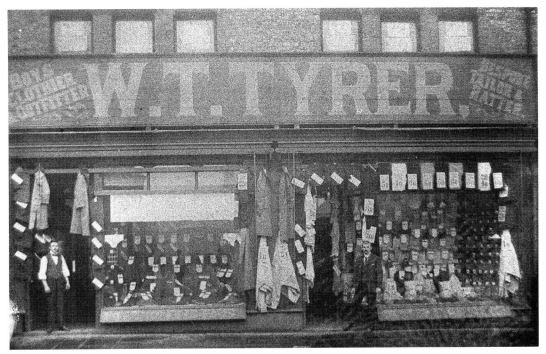

136 In 1881, 14-year-old William Tinsley Tyrer was working for Dromgoole as an apprentice printer. The ink gave him a skin rash and his employer transferred him to his Liverpool Road clothing business. Seven years later, at 12 Liverpool Road, William T. Tyrer opened his own men's outfitters. He and his brother Richard (left) are seen here *c.*1898 outside 12-14 Liverpool Road— already by then a good quality, male only emporium.

137 By 1938 Tyrers was celebrating its Golden Jubilee—aided here by the Haydock Brass Band. The firm had expanded into neighbouring premises, now sold ladies' fashions and was justly proud of its re-modelled frontage and interior. Road-widening caused a move to Bridge Street where Tyrers' new store opened on 23 November 1960.

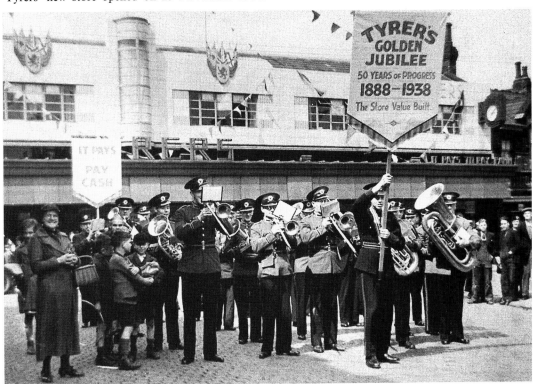

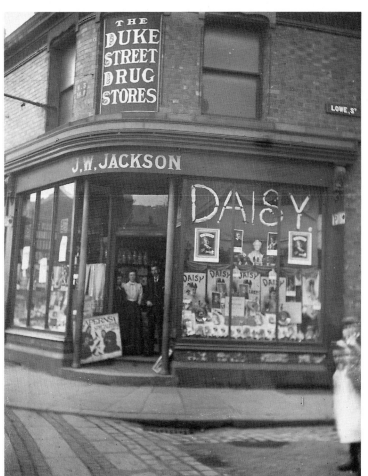

138 Jabez W. Jackson's business as chemist and druggist at 107 Higher Parr Street prospered and branches were set up, including this one at the corner of Duke Street and Lowe Street. What prompted the 'Daisy' display? Posters and photographs certainly dominate, leaving the traditional tall jars and chemists' wares to form a faint background on the shelves at the rear of the shop.

139 Walter Jackson, Jabez's son, was an enthusiastic photographer of neighbourhood events as well as of his family's shops. (He was also secretary of Holy Trinity Cycling Club when it was formed in 1902.) Here, thanks to his delayed-action camera, he stands to the right of the group, his smartness contrasting with the barefoot boy on the left. There were local charitable distributions of bread, and this is one. The cart belongs to Frank Houlton, a Higher Parr Street grocer, and one wonders if, though laden, it held sufficient for the queue of shawl-clad women, children and nuns.

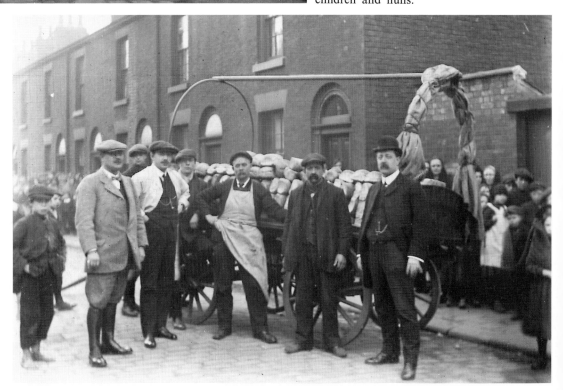

140 Walter's photography had to be outdoor, sometimes with a curtain or sheet as back-cloth and a pot-plant to lend elegance. At this Jackson wedding (brides were not yet wearing white) those immediately concerned are shown in the back yard.

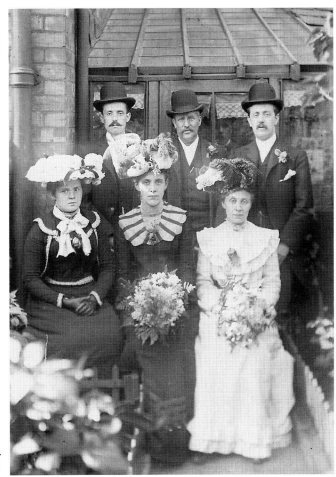

141 To accommodate the whole family group, including Walter's wife (top row, left) and two of his children, the party had to pose in the back entry!

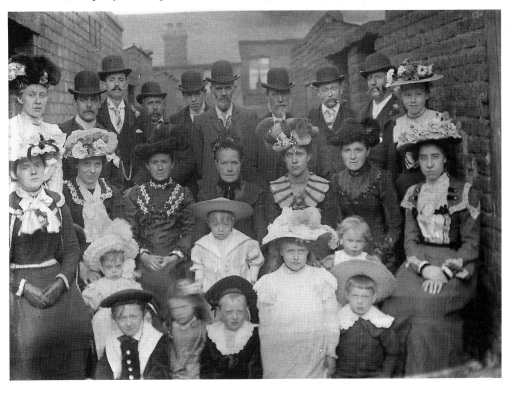

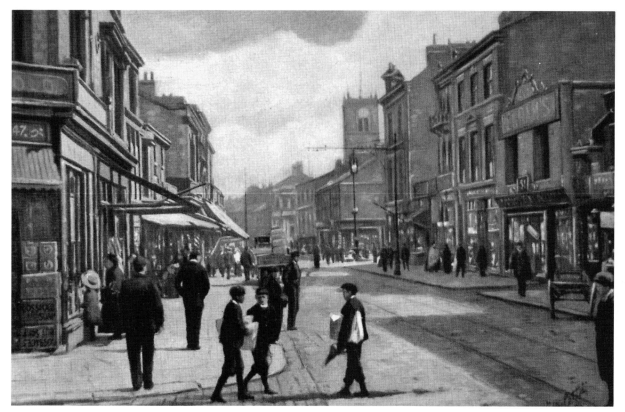

142 Viewed from the corner of Hardshaw Street, early 20th-century Church Street is bathed in summer sun. Shop blinds are extended to shade the wares and at no.47 newly delivered goods stand in the doorway, including Gossage's Soap. Newsboys are setting off. The Parish Church tower and its north aisle wall are visible and beyond is the bright stonework of the Post Office.

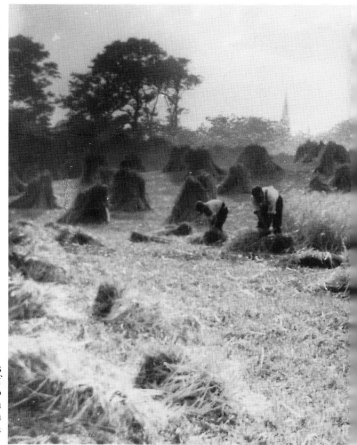

143 The spire of Christ Church, Eccleston, shows this former field to be well to the Windle side of Chapel Lane. Harvesters are using twisted stalks to bind the cut barley into sheaves, some of which have already been stooked to dry. With no sickle in sight, the long-stalked crop appears to be cut by a mechanical reaper pulled by the pair of horses.

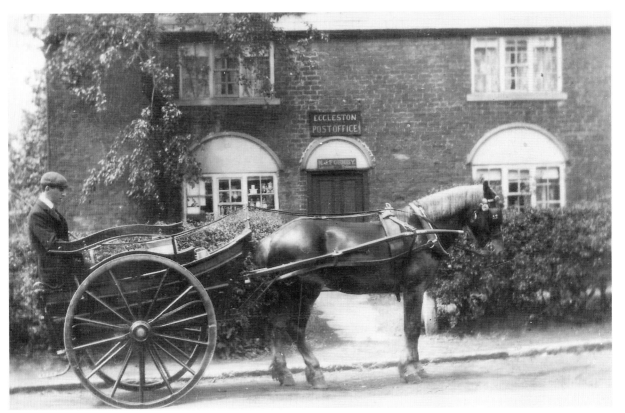

144 When in 1956 Christ Church Eccleston's 19th-century vicarage was demolished, the stone inscribed with the griffin and the kingfisher crests of Samuel Taylor and his wife was incorporated in the new building. Across the road, on the corner of Church Lane and Springfield Lane, the days of Eccleston Post Office (then usually called Chorley's) and its tall pear tree were numbered. Here *c.*1910 James Cook of Knowles House Farm has paused outside the Post Office in his milk float. Note the large churn from which milk was sold, being poured into customers' jugs from measures kept in the smaller container.

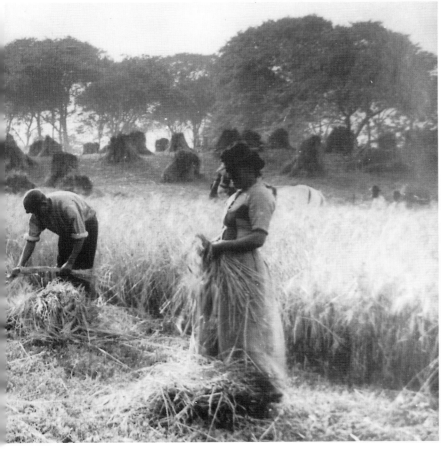

Stage and Screen

145 Set at the corner of Milk Street and Waterloo Street, this building was from 1861-90 St Helens' second Theatre Royal. The first had been a simple wooden building erected at the foot of Bridge Street in 1847. Inside, the new theatre's elegantly curving dress circle seemed more Georgian than Victorian and survived the building's years of Salvation Army use. Now, as the 'Citadel', the building is again a performing arts venue.

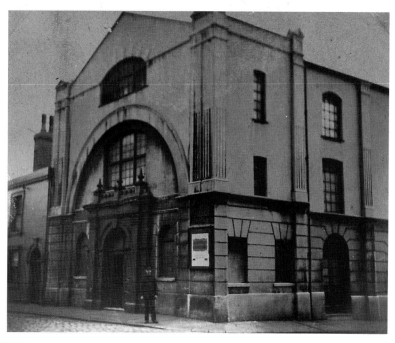

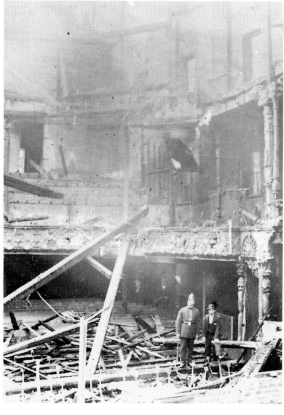

146 This photograph reveals the fate of St Helens' third Theatre Royal—an elaborate building designed by Frank Matcham—which had opened on Corporation Street in August 1890. Initially successful, by December 1898 when its manager died suddenly profits were flagging. Ten months later fire devastated the theatre. Here, in the aftermath, workmen and a police constable/fireman stand facing the stage in the gutted auditorium.

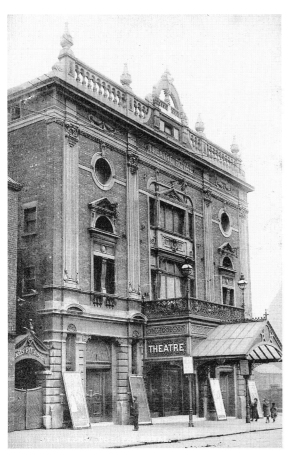

147 Thanks to David Gamble, Frederick Dixon-Nuttall and Joseph Beecham (then Mayor), the ruins were bought and the theatre, whose facade and walls had survived, was reconstructed —'The determination', wrote Beecham's obituarist, 'being to supply the town with first rate drama and to cultivate a taste for the best things in music.' With its interior layout improved and electric lighting installed, the Theatre Royal (seen here *c*.1910) re-opened on 20 May 1901.

148 Further along Corporation Street the People's Palace, a large wooden structure seating 2,000, opened as a variety theatre in April 1893. It prospered and, re-built to this design, re-opened in 1903 as the Hippodrome. Ten years later both gallery and circle were raised and re-aligned to allow films to be projected. Both live and cinematograph performances were given. One thrill for the young was the personal appearance of the cowboy film hero Eddie Polo, brandishing and firing pistols—but disappointingly short in stature.

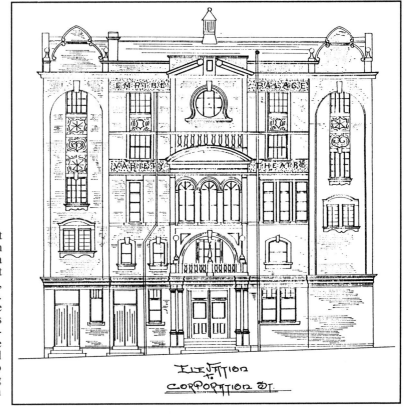

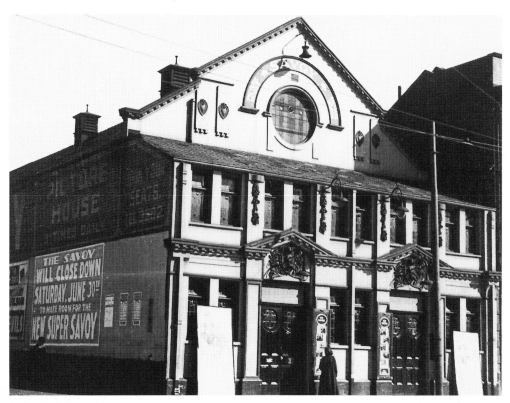

149 St Helens' first three cinemas, which all opened towards the end of 1911, included Griffins Picture Theatre, Ormskirk Street and the Parrvilion [sic], Jackson Street. Here, in Bridge Street, *The Beehive* was demolished to make way for the third, the Picturedrome, at the corner of Exchange Street. Later renamed the Savoy, it had 520 seats, and is seen here shortly before it closed and further demolition could take place.

150 The first of the eight months taken to build the new Savoy Luxury Theatre was spent driving piles 30ft. deep into the poor subsoil. It opened on 25 March 1935 with the Mayor, Councillor O'Brien, presiding. The main film shown in the spacious air-conditioned cinema was *The House of Rothschild* starring George Arliss. Prices ranged from 7d. (3p) to 1s. 6d. (7½p) for its 1,467 seats, some of which were fitted with hearing aids.

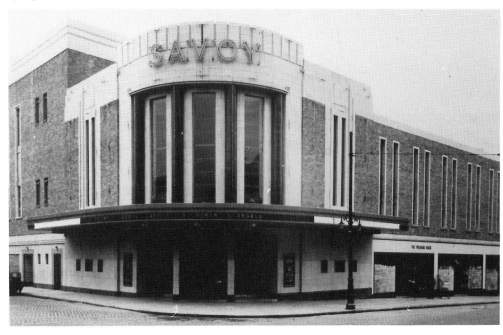

Things to Celebrate

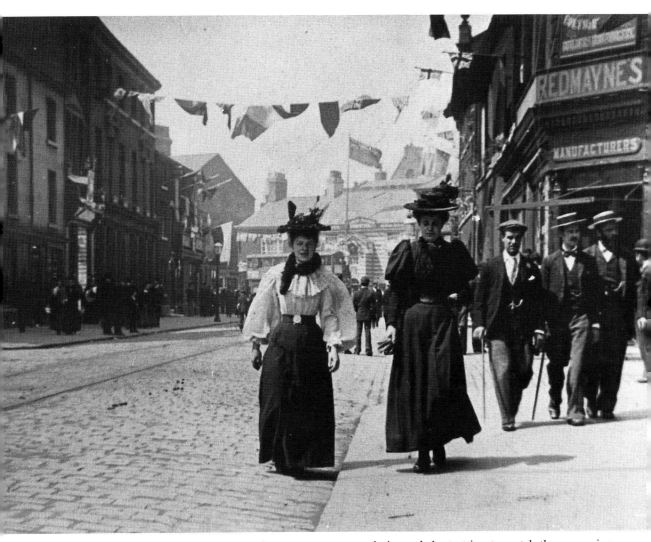

151 Jubilee Day, 22 June 1897, was an occasion to step out smartly in one's best attire, to watch the procession led by 160 mounted white-coated butchers head for Grange Park, and to enjoy the flag-decked streets and buildings, like these in Church Street. Had the townsfolk here heard St Thomas's bells welcome the day at midnight and the sporadic nocturnal explosion of works' detonators? Did they join the crowds at Grange Park, or save their energies for the evening's grand display of fireworks off Bishop Road?

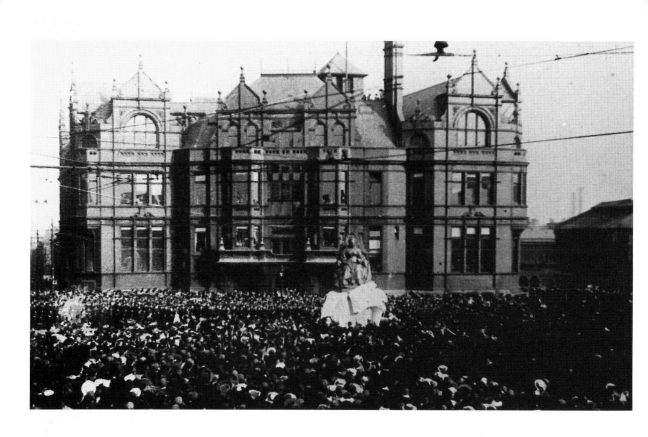
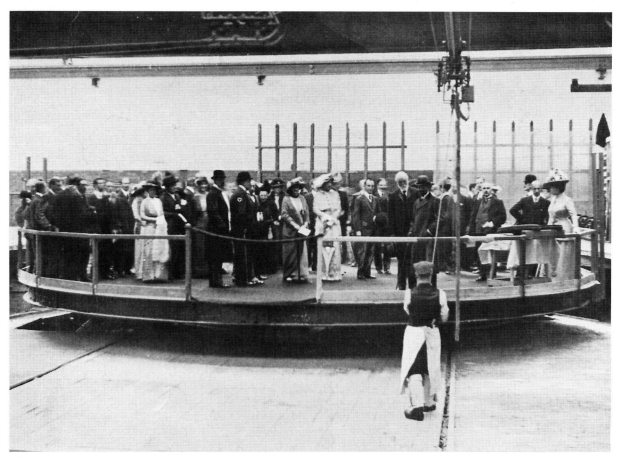

152 (*top left*) There was no room for trams (whose overhead wires can be seen) when crowds packed the now completed, and about to be re-named, Town Hall Square on 14 April 1905 to see the Earl of Derby unveil the bronze statue of Queen Victoria given to the town by William Windle Pilkington. Previously, to bring this through the archway from the station goods yard, it had proved necessary temporarily to lower the roadway. As recommended by the sculptor, George G. Frampton, the monarch then had the massive Gamble Insitute as a backcloth and looked out towards the Y.M.C.A.

153 (*bottom left*) When King George V and Queen Mary visited St Helens on 8 July 1913 they were honoured guests at Pilkington's Cowley Hill works. The official party can be seen here on a 35ft-wide mobile Malevez disc with added railings. William Windle Pilkington stands with the bowler-hatted king.

Usually the disc was close-packed with glass that had been 'swum' (rhythmically trodden) into a quick-setting plaster of Paris bed. Then it was moved along the rails to be automatically ground and polished.

On leaving, the royal visitors entered Victoria Park's specially built King's Gate before driving between crowds of flag-waving cheering school children to the Bishop Road gateway en route to Southport.

154 Simon the dog seems to have pride of place in this photograph of the party in Atherton Street in honour of Elizabeth II's coronation. All had fun, but some small ones standing here look bemused. Were the flag-decked street and the bigger children's fancy dress too much for them? With due dignity a be-spectacled lad reverently holds a replica of the Queen's coronation crown.

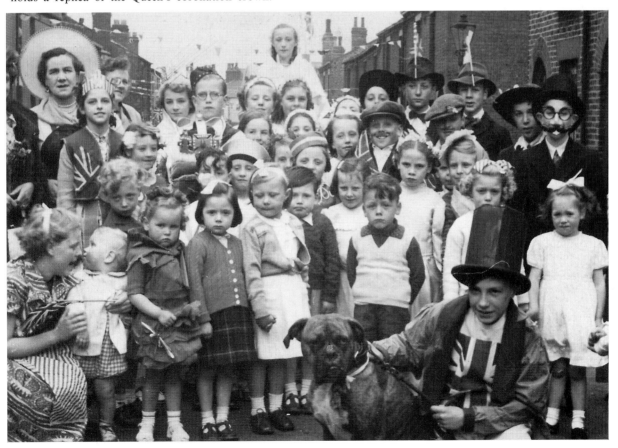

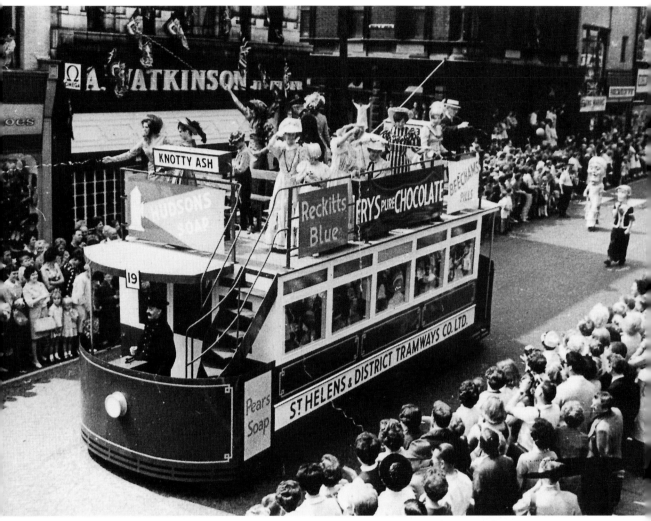

155 Purists will contend that no St Helens tram ever looked like this one. Created on a lorry chassis at the Corporation's Hardshaw Brook Depot, it delighted its passengers and the crowds who had assembled on Saturday 27 July 1968 to watch the grand parade held to celebrate St Helens' centenary as a borough. Here the procession is moving along Church Street towards its destination at Sherdley Park and has just passed Naylor Street.

From the success of these celebrations evolved the St Helens Show, a major three-day event held each summer in Sherdley Park.

At Leisure

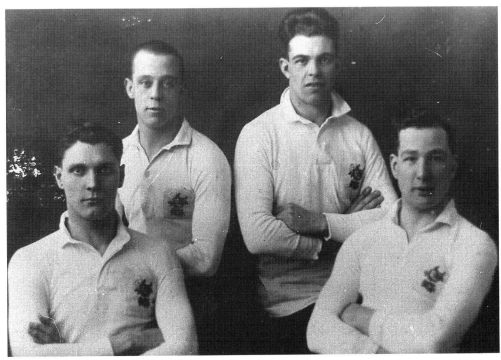

156 In 1874 at the town's first recorded rugby match a 20-strong St Helens team lost to a rather smaller one from Liverpool Royal Infirmary. From that beginning the 'Saints' (St Helens Rugby League Football Club) evolved. This quartet of 1930s team members (Fairclough, Frodsham, Ellaby and Halfpenny) were together selected for the Great Britain squad.

157 As usual, Saints' Knowsley Road ground was packed for the annual trial of strength with arch rivals Wigan shown in this 1960s photograph. Alex Murphy has the ball and to his left is Eric Ashton, then captaining Wigan and now a Saints' director.

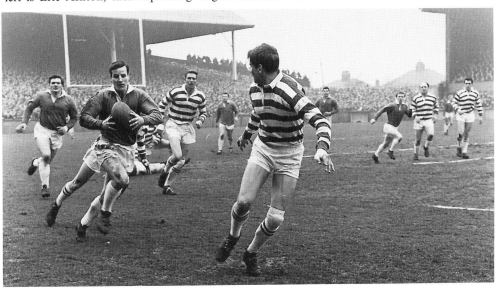

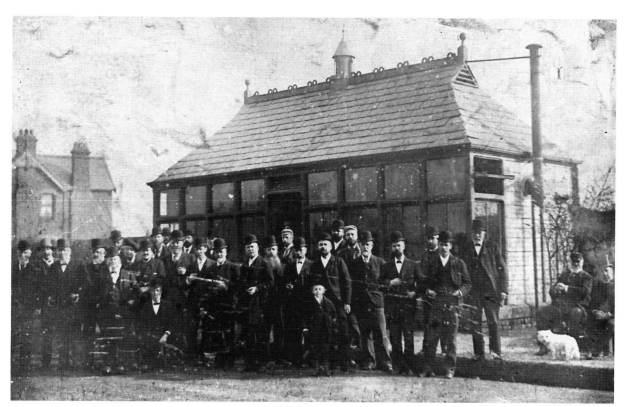

158 St Helens' Bowling Club was established at the end of Regents Road in the fashionable Queen's Park/St Ann's district in 1880. How many of the members in this early 1900s group in front of their pavilion were among the 65 who paid one shilling (5p) each in 1882 for keys to the door.

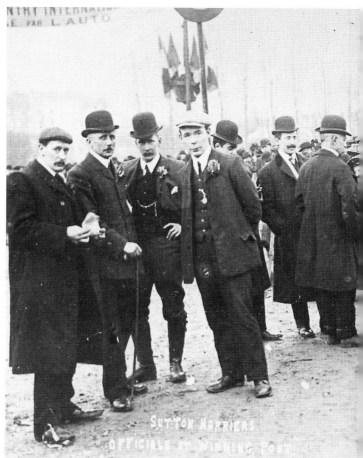

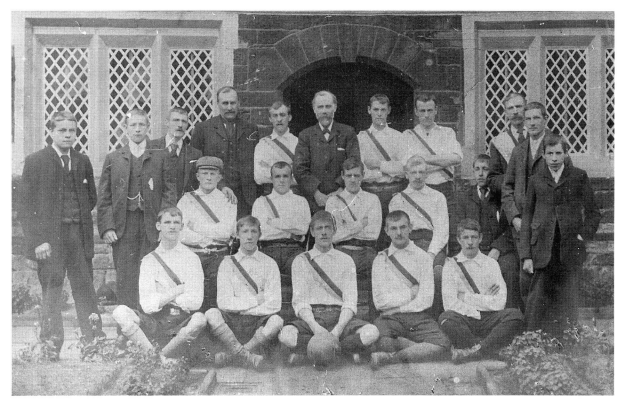

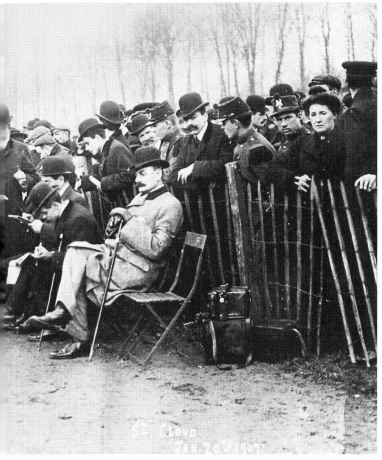

159 Early this century the St Helens and District Sunday School Football League was flourishing. In 1908 Nutgrove were fielding teams in Divisions 1 and 2. St Thomas's won the League's handsome shield in 1910. This undated photograph from the Friends Meeting House shows a Quaker team and its supporters. Extreme right stands Edward Kenyon, whose grandson copied the photograph. As with the other teams, these players seem somewhat mature 'Sunday Scholars'.

160 In 1906, seven years after their formation, Sutton Harriers and Athletic Club won the English National Championship. Invited to compete in an international event at St Cloud, Paris, in January 1907, they proved the successful team. Clustered near the winning post that day are four Harriers' officials, about to be surprised by the fluent French of their immaculate President, Captain Michael Hughes, seated at the right.

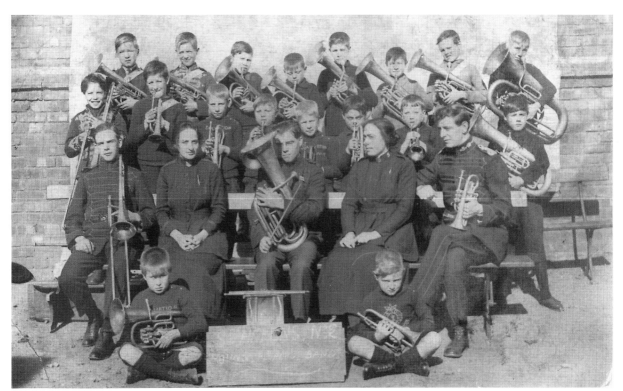

161 Frequently to be heard, bands practised, paraded, competed, supported local events and performed in the parks. Usually attached to churches, collieries and other works, the bandsmen might well start young, like the members of the Salvation Army No.2 Youth Band.

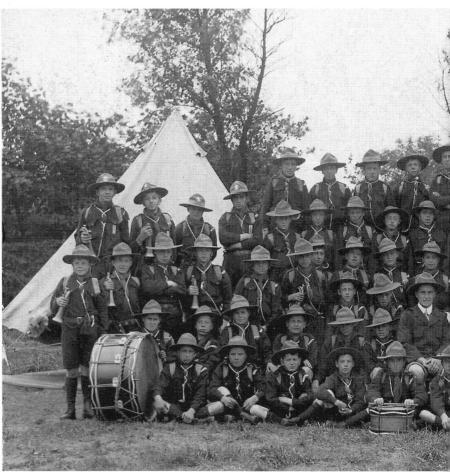

162 Founded in 1884, St Helens Y.M.C.A moved from the Ragged School to Hardshaw Street before being given the old Congregational manse in College Street by Col. W. Windle Pilkington. Beside this their gymnasium (towards which Queen Victoria's statue originally faced) was built in 1890. Next door, on 15 October 1903, the Earl of Aberdeen opened this Ruabon brick and terracotta Briggs and Wolstenholme building. Above its street level shops were a library, reading, lecture, refreshment, games and dark rooms, and even a roof garden. A wide Cannington-Shaw bottle, containing 1902 newspapers and memorabilia, inserted above the foundation stone laid by Col. Pilkington, has been retrieved intact during recent alterations.

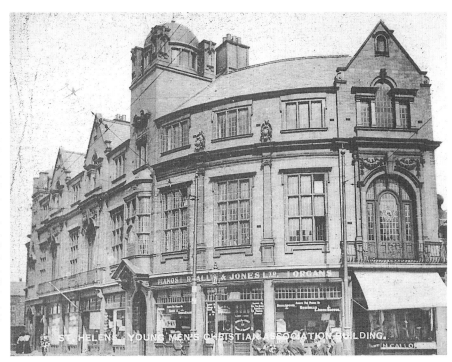

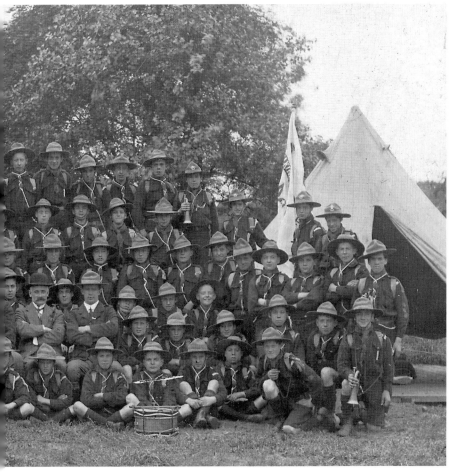

163 The 1st St Helens YMCA Scout troop, though not registered officially until 1910, in fact dates from March 1908, and can now claim to be the oldest still in existence in the country. Its foundation followed Scouting's public inauguration at a meeting in Birkenhead on 24 January 1908 addressed by Baden-Powell. Two days later he spoke at the YMCA, St Helens. Tommy Cousins was the first Patrol leader and John Pennington, the builder, was Scoutmaster. This was the troop by 1910—seen at camp, and obviously with its own band.

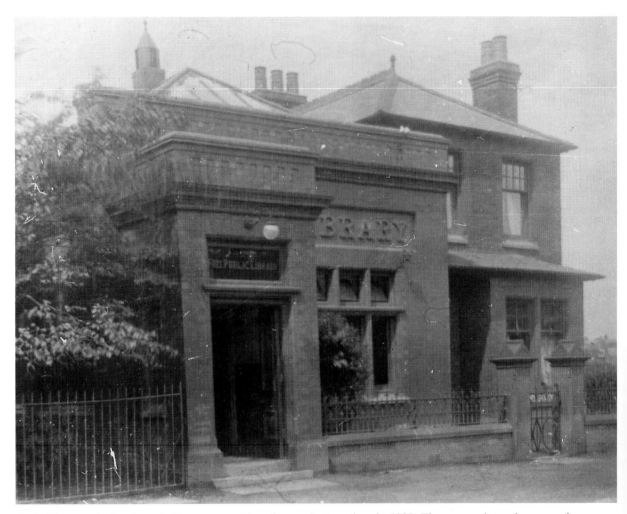

164 The town's first branch library opened in a former Sutton shop in 1887. Three years later these premises were built on Thatto Heath Road. After 1915 when the present library was built, thanks to a £3,000 grant from Andrew Carnegie, the earlier building became a police station. It is now the Borough's Thatto Heath Local Office. Appropriately, when the road to its left was created, it was named Lacey Street [124].

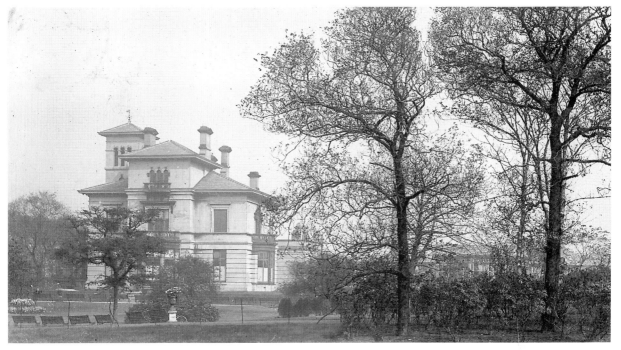

165 John Ansdell (1803-85), prospering as a solicitor, in 1851 quit his large Greenbank home and brought his family to Cowley House new-built for him by George Harris. As Clerk to the County Court, Secretary and later Chairman of the Gas Light Company, negotiator of property deals and shrewd purchaser of land and property to rent, he did well. After his death his widow moved to Rainhill and all was sold, items auctioned revealing the Ansdells' prosperous lifestyle. Bought by the Borough, within months the grounds had become Cowley Hill Park, and in 1892 Andsdell's home became the town's museum.

166 When Victoria's Golden Jubilee was celebrated in June 1887 the new park was ceremoniously re-named Victoria Park by David Gamble. His gift of land made access to the park possible from North Road. The Ansdells had approached from the Bishop Road/Cowley Hill Lane entrance.

St Mark's Gate and adjoining lodge are seen here in their early days. Behind to the right is St Mark's Church, built in 1883 to James Gandy's design, and also funded by David Gamble.

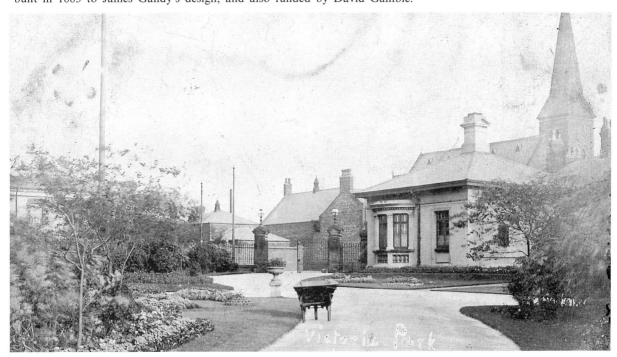

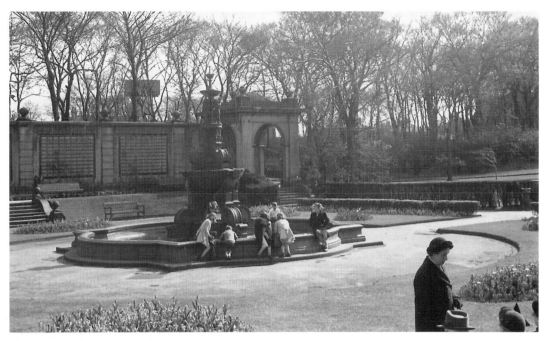

167 Victoria Park and the museum quickly became popular venues. The formal gardens near the house were enhanced by the terracotta fountains presented by Sir Henry Doulton [27]. Erected in May 1897, it was stocked with 60 goldfish by the Angling Association. Children, however, were not to walk on the grass verges nor, as they could in this Easter 1957 scene, to play or loiter near the fountain. All could visit the museum—whose long-departed stuffed tiger many remember—until 1966 saw the transfer of the exhibits to the Gamble Institute.

168 Formed by damming the Black Brook, and enlarged and deepened over the years, Carr Mill Dam supplied water to the canal via its Blackbrook branch. Over the years the dam has been sailed, fished, swum, in bitter winters skated upon, picnicked beside, and walked around. Sadly, only traces remain of the model railway that in the 1950s was a magnet for the young—attracted also by the roller-skating rink and the fine helter-skelter that stood near the present *Waterside*.

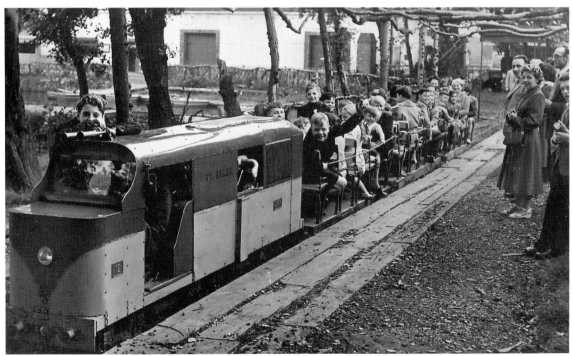

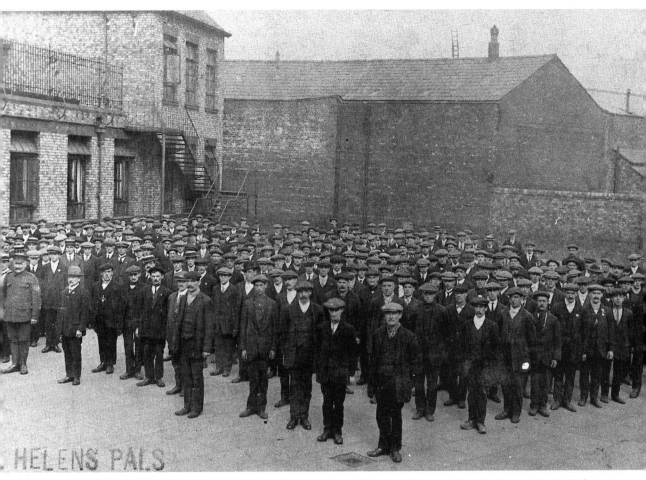

169   Three days' intensive recruiting created the 11th Battalion of the South Lancashire Regiment, the St Helens 'Pals'. Many of the 1,000 who signed on are mustered here in a College Street school yard a day later, 4 September 1914, their feet already planted army-style.

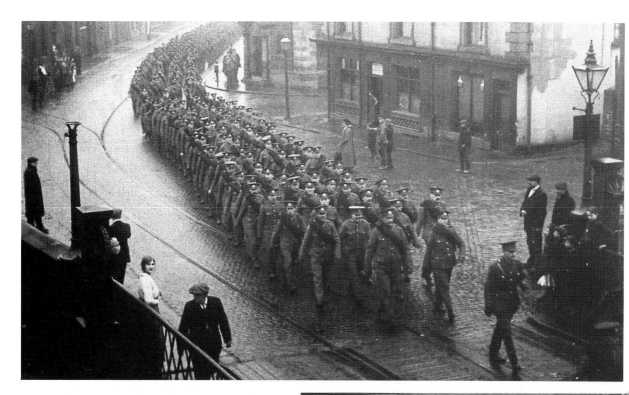

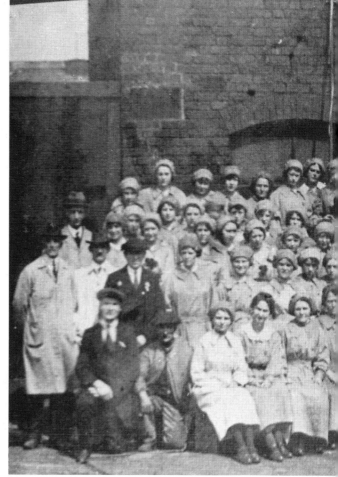

170 Five months later, clad in the grey uniforms provided by the Borough Council (khaki came in later), and ready to leave for training at Bangor, the 'Pals' march briskly to church parade. They have come from their makeshift barracks in the former Sutton Oak glassworks via Peasley Cross. The foremost are about to cross the lift bridge over the canal [25] and enter Church Street. The 'Pals' reached the Western Front in November 1915 and were involved, with considerable losses, in both battles of the Somme, and at Passchendale.

171 In both world wars Forster's engineering departments at Atlas Street turned to shell-making, and in the First World War a Ministry of Munitions depot occupied vacant buildings at Pocket Nook, later to be bought by Forsters. Another depot, at the former glass works at Sutton Oak, seems Store 34's most likely location. The differently coloured overalls of the largely female workforce revealed at once which task each performed.

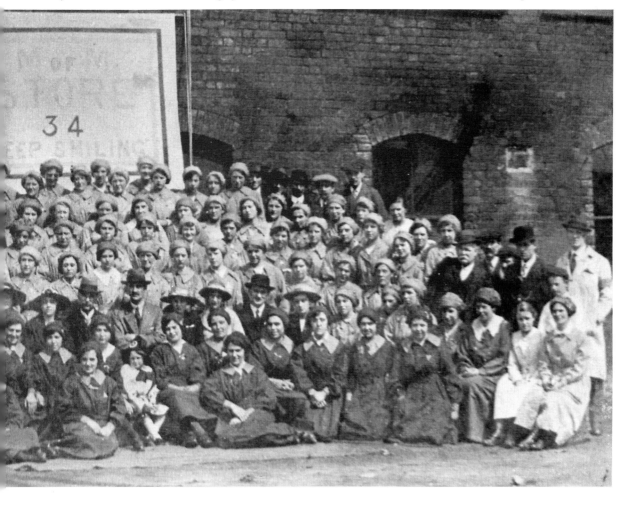

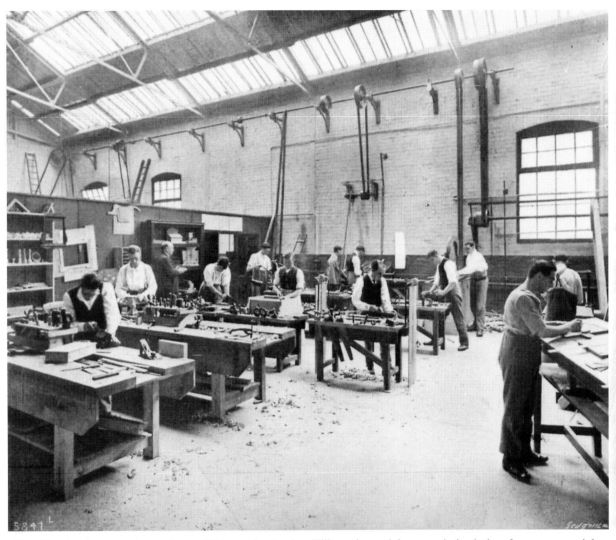

172 Munitions were also made at Pilkington's Cowley Hill works and income derived therefrom was used by Pilkington to provide a special hospital within the Ravenhead works for convalescent other ranks. This opened in January 1917 with Dr. J.R. Kerr, the firm's medical officer, in charge. He was experienced in both industrial injuries and French therapeutic techniques for disabled servicemen.

Acquiring workshop skills complemented more customary orthopaedic treatments. Tools and tasks, as here in the woodwork shop, were adapted to individual needs.

The hospital closed in 1925. Subsequently part became the Ravenhead Theatre—much used for amateur dramatic performances and concerts, including several Boy Scout Gang Shows.

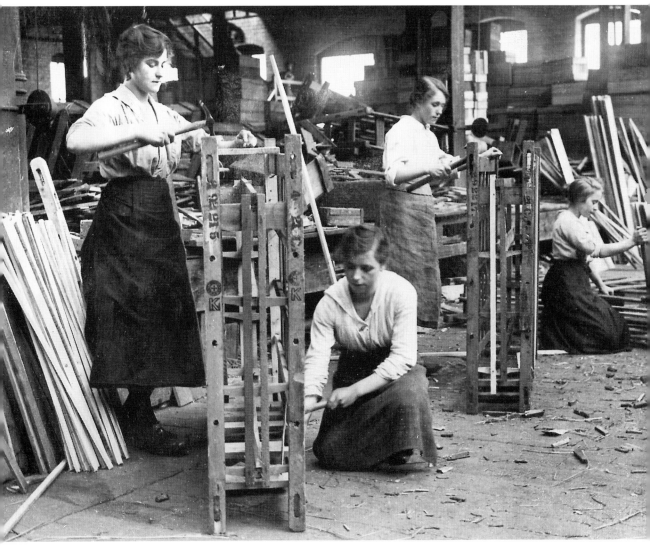

173 As men left for the forces rôles changed at Pilkington. Boy Scouts helped man the fire brigade. Some women puddled brick clay. Others, as here, were kept busy repairing the crates in which glass was despatched.

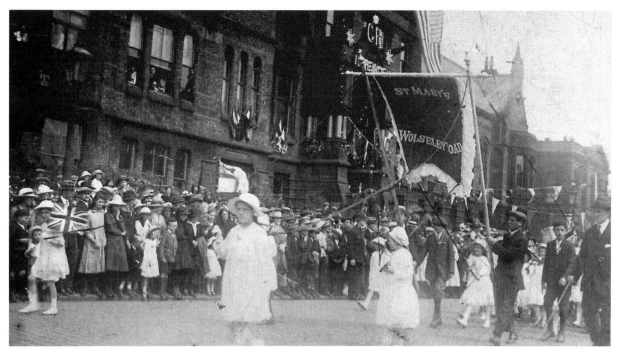

174 The ending of hostilities in November 1918 was officially celebrated by a formal procession on Peace Day, 15 July 1919. As on many local occasions, banners were carried. Seen here passing the crowd gathered at the Town Hall is a party from St Mary's mission church and school in Wolseley Road.

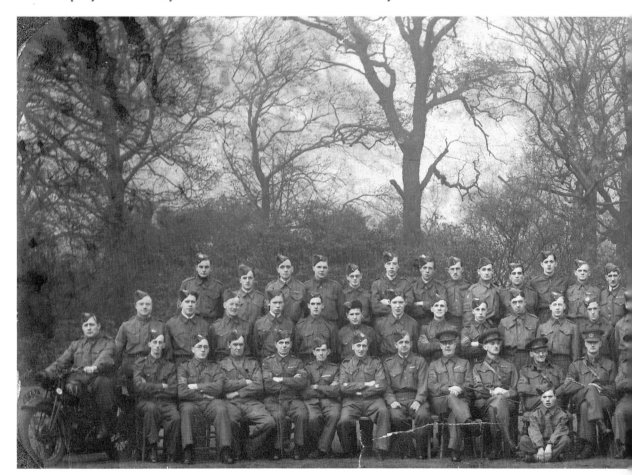

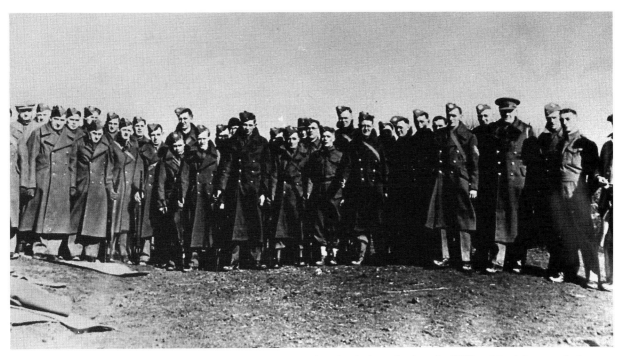

175 This picture of Forster's Home Guard Company, taken in their early days in 1941, with eight guns between them, may call to mind 'Dad's Army'.

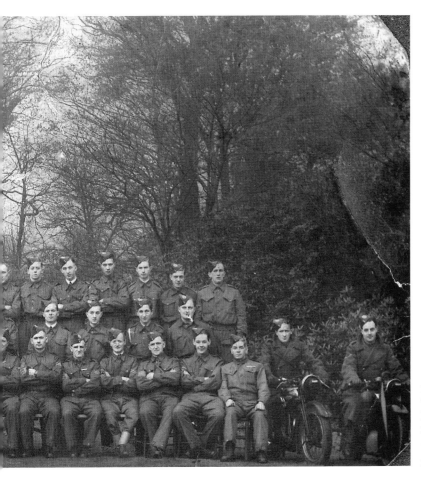

176 By 1942, when Sherdley Park 'C' Company based at Sherdley Hall were photographed, time seems to have allowed the Home Guard to become better organised. Their C.O., Captain Hamilton, sits at the centre, with their mascot, young Hadley, at his feet.

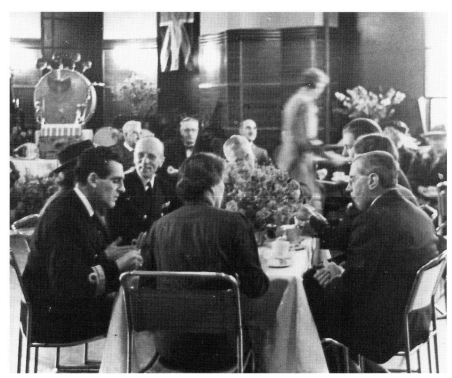

177 Soon after St Helens adopted HMS *Myrmidon* in Warships' Week 1942, the destroyer was given to the Polish navy. Now re-named O.R.P. *Orkan* she brought General Sikorski's body back from Gibraltar. Some months after a brief visit to St Helens, her commander and two fellow officers returned in August 1943 for a formal exchange of plaques at the Town Hall.

The illustration shows them being entertained that afternoon by the W.V.S. at the gaslit Gas Showrooms, where they accepted the musical instruments (background left) provided by the W.V.S. for the ship's company.

The two W.V.S. members delivering the instruments were permitted to tour O.R.P. *Orkan*, having been described to dock security by the officers as 'our godmothers'.

178 St Helens led the way in post-war reconciliation. In 1948 the Mayor and Town Clerk made a goodwill visit to Stuttgart. Welcomed by the Oberburgermeister, Field-Marshal Rommel's son, they saw how the city was reconstructing itself from its rubble while many citizens existed in appalling conditions. Exchange visits began and, in 1951, this party from Stuttgart are surveying their partner-town from the tower of Lowe House. Extending its links with Europe, St Helens was officially twinned with Chalon-sur-Saône in 1964.

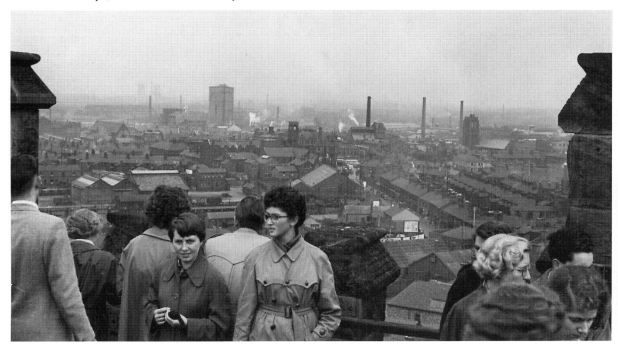

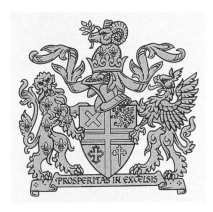

Towards 'Prosperitas in Excelsis'

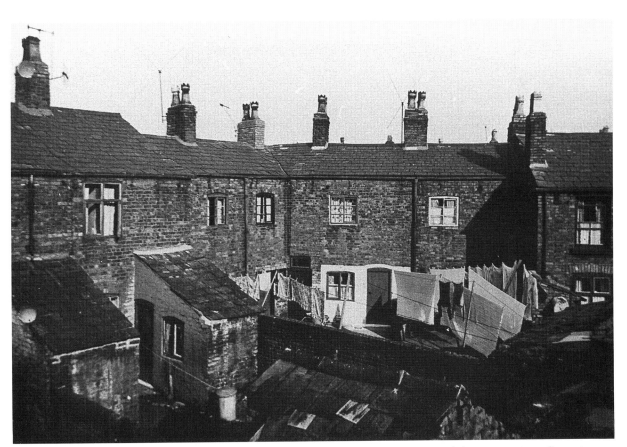

179 By the late 1950s renewal and redevelopment, hindered by the war, were gaining momentum. Soon to go would be these houses at the corner of Ashcroft Street and Higher Parr Street, where washing lines converge across the back yards. Neat whitewash surrounds a traditional window, opened by sliding one half behind the other along horizontal grooves. TV had arrived, but was there indoor sanitation?

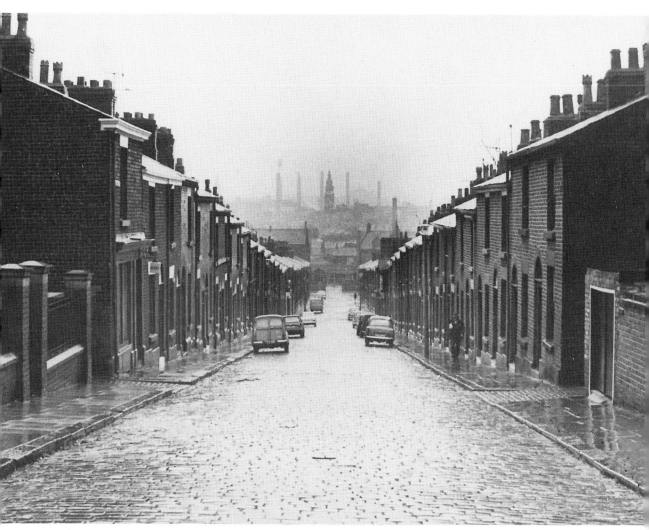

180 Change was imminent for Morley Street, seen here in the early 1960s after rain. Its whitened door steps stand out more clearly than Lowe House School at the foot of the hill and Beecham's distant clock tower.

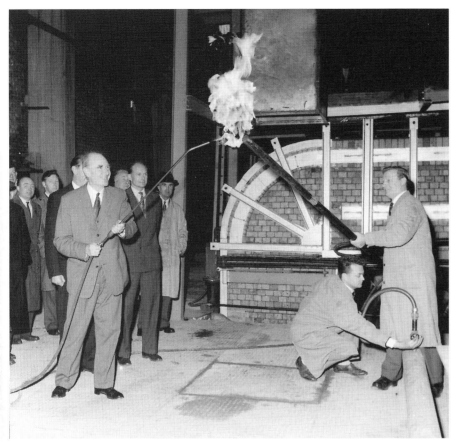

181 Dramatic change came to flat glassmaking with the development of float glass. Having progressed from the tank on to a bath of molten tin, when cooled the glass was smooth and clear. Produced in various thicknesses it supplanted sheet and plate glass. Sir Harry (later Lord) Pilkington, who announced the new product in January 1959, is here three years later firing Cowley Hill 3 float tank (Alastair Pilkington, 'inventor' of float glass, stands at his left). Chairman of Pilkington 1949-73, and noted for cycling on business through the City of London, Sir Harry was a familiar and respected St Helenian who did much for the town and who became a prominent national figure. On his death in 1983 he was much missed both locally and nationally.

182 Long overdue, since technical education classes had for years overflowed from the Gamble Institute into many other buildings, the new Technical College, variously named, began to take shape in Water Street in the late 1950s. First built was the block to the left, opened in 1958. This expanded in a rearward branch from which the range in the background sprouted, topped by the library. Newest arrival in this early 1970s photograph is the block on stilts which nowadays has grown a fire-escape staircase. Evening classes account for the blaze of lights.

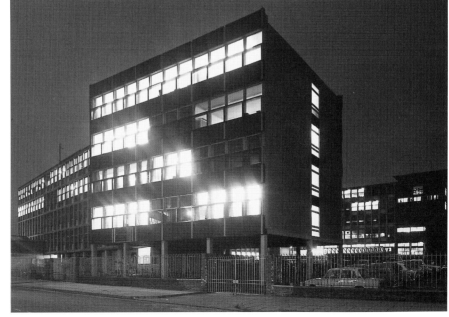

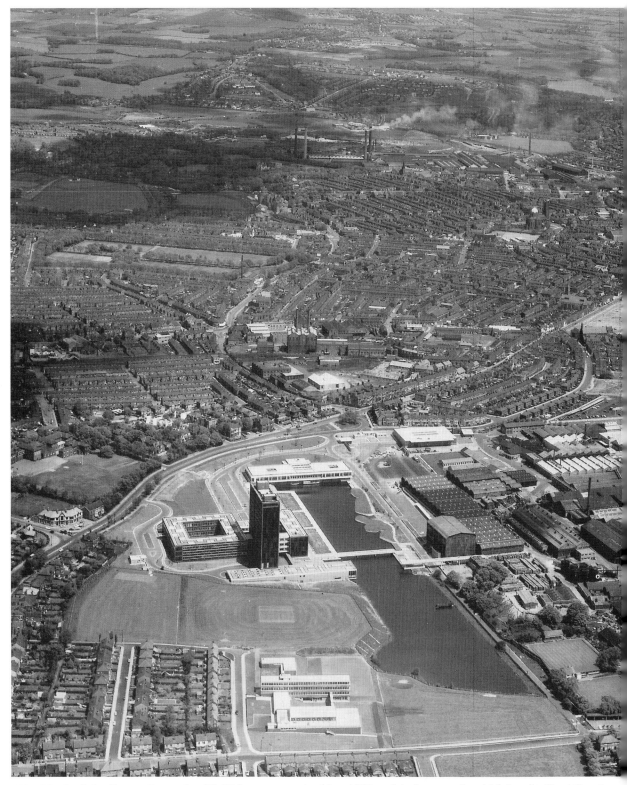

183 Much of the County Borough of St Helens appears in this *c*.1970 aerial photograph, which has Stafford Road and Factory Row running across the foreground. Change is imminent. The boundaries of the 1974 Metropolitan Borough will extend to distant Billinge and Haydock. Landmarks like Stafford Road's Edmund Campion School, and the power station left of centre will disappear. New housing will occupy many surrounding fields and, in the 1990s, reclamation of the area on the extreme right, halfway up the picture, will reveal the ancient coal workings [3].

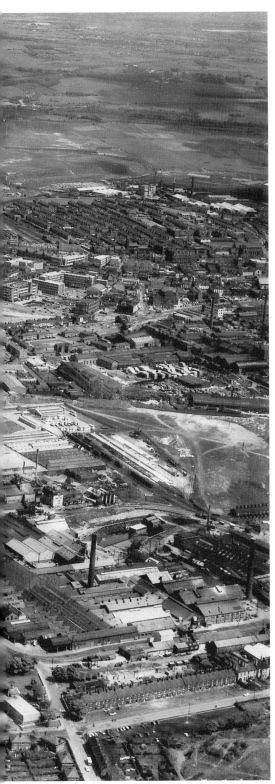

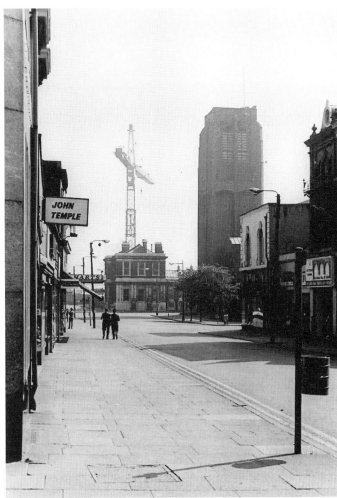

184 Redevelopment and renewal were under way when Church Street was photographed by Wallace Collins early in the 1970s and the crane was becoming a familiar sight. St Mary's Market complex was being constructed, and the Post Office, centre background, would vanish next. It and the balconied three-storeyed shop on the right were also present in illustration [142]. The Parish Church, whose impressive tower dominates the background, would survive—but in much altered surroundings.

Bibliography

Access to H.E. Course, 'The Elusive Bromilows', St Helens College (1992)

Anon., *Christ Church Eccleston*, privately published (1988)

Anon., *Industries of Lancashire: Part Second*, Historical Publishing Company (1889)

Anon., *Rockware Glass St Helens*, company publication (*c*.1975)

Anon., *St Helens Commercially Considered*, St Helens Corporation (1935)

Aspin, C., *Lancashire, the First Industrial Society*, Helmshore Local History Society (1969)

Bagley, J.J., *A History of Lancashire*, Phillimore (1976)

Bagley, J.J., *Lancashire Diarists*, Phillimore (1975)

Bagley, J.J. and Hodgkiss, A.G., *Lancashire: A History of the County Palatine in Early Maps*, Neil Richardson (1985)

Baines, E., *History, Directory and Gazetteer of the County Palatine of Lancaster*, Wm. Wales & Co. (1825)

Barker, T.C., *An Age of Glass*, Boxtree (1994)

Barker, T.C., *Lancashire Coal, Cheshire Salt & the Rise of Liverpool*, Transactions of the Historic Society of Lancashire & Cheshire (1951)

Barker, T.C., *Pilkington Brothers and the Glass Industry*, Allen & Unwin (1960)

Barker, T.C., *The Glassmakers*, Weidenfeld and Nicolson (1977)

Barker, T.C., *The Sankey Navigation*, Transactions of the Historic Society of Lancashire & Cheshire (1950)

Barker, T.C. and Harris, J.R., *A Merseyside Town in the Industrial Revolution: St Helens 1750-1900*, Cass (1993)

Bradshaw, G., *Hand-Book to the Manufacturing Districts of Great Britain* (1854)

Brockbank, J., *History of St Helens with Local Landmarks*, Wood and Co. (1896)

Chaloner, W.H., *Palatinate Studies: V—Salt in Cheshire*, Chetham Society (1992)

Fairclough, H.L., *A Centenary Record*, Grange Park Golf Club (1991)

Giblin, J.F., *The Churches of St Helens*, privately published (1995)

Gray, T., *St Helens as a Manufacturing Centre*, Magazine of Commerce (1908)

Harley, J.B., *William Yates's Map of Lancashire 1786*, Historic Society of Lancashire and Cheshire (1968)

Harris, S.A., *Henry Berry: Liverpool's Second Dock Engineer*, Transactions of the Historic Society of Lancashire & Cheshire (1938)

Henderson, Tom, *A Short History of St Helens Parish*, privately published (*c*.1976)

Lazenby, W., *Thrice Happy Place: Ormskirk Street Congregational Church*, privately published (1972)

Mills, D., *The Place Names of Lancashire*, Batsford (1976)

Morris, R.J.B., *A Short History of St Helens Parks*, privately published (1976)

Moss, H. *et al.*, *History of Forster's Glass Co. Ltd.*, company publication (*c*.1966)

Pevsner, N., *South Lancashire* Penguin (1969)

Rees, P., *A Guide to the Industrial Heritage of Merseyside* NWSIAH (1978)

Simm, G. and Winstanley, I., *Mining Memories*, St Helens MBC (1990)

Singleton, D., *Liverpool and Manchester Railway*, Dalesman Books (1975)

Taylor, K.T., *The Cowley Schools*, St Helens MBC (1987)

Tolson, J.M., *The St Helens Railway*, Oakwood Press (1983)

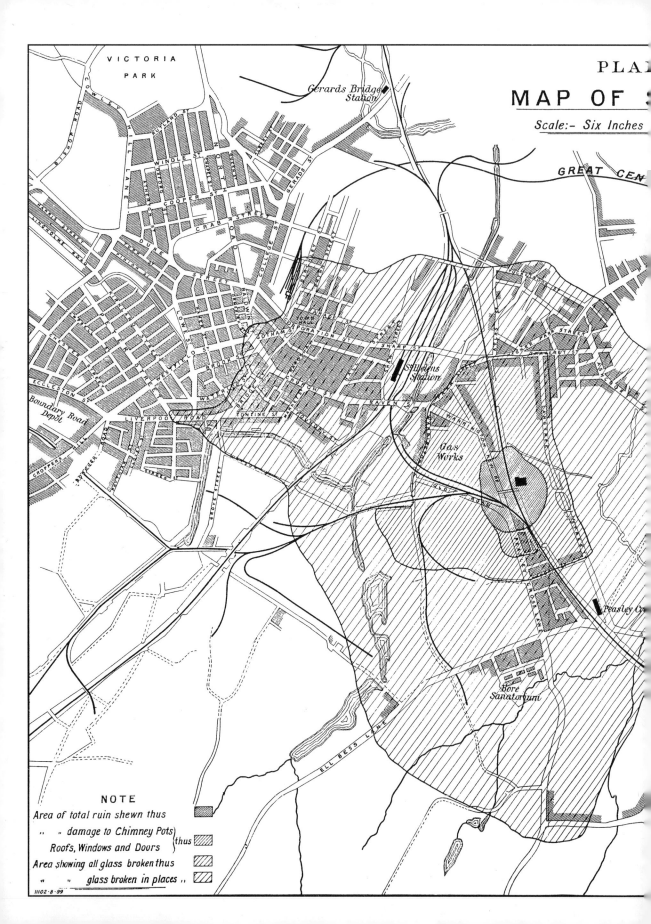

PLAN

MAP OF S

Scale:- Six Inches

VICTORIA PARK

Gerards Bridge Station

GREAT CEN

St Helens Station

Gas Works

Boundary Road Depot

Bore Sanatorium

Peasley Cr

NOTE

Area of total ruin shewn thus

 "   " damage to Chimney Pots }
Roofs, Windows and Doors } thus

Area showing all glass broken thus

 "   " glass broken in places "

11102·8·99